DISCOV

UTTLESFORD

Circular Walks along The Uttlesford Way in Essex

Peter Cooper

Designed & Edited by Jacqueline Cooper
Maps by Carol Wilkinson
Photographs by P. & J. Cooper

Further copies from: 24 Pelham Road, Clavering, Saffron Walden, Essex CB11 4PQ
Enquiries: peterg.cooper@virgin.net

Introduction

The Uttlesford District of N.W. Essex boasts a diversity of countryside and proves the lie to the commonly held idea that Essex is flat. The highest point in the county may be only 450 feet above sea level, but that does not mean the countryside is boring. In fact it is very varied and interesting. In the 16 walks described in this book you will enjoy many fine views in this undulating part of the county. You will visit pretty villages, walk in woods, stroll beside rivers and through fields of corn, explore unspoilt country lanes and see many historic buildings, and at the end of most walks you can enjoy a drink in a country pub. This is a quiet, thinly-populated area where wildlife is abundant. Rabbits, pheasants and partridges will run ahead of you, whilst finches and other small birds fly between branches. If it is quiet you may see deer (fallow, roe and muntjac are plentiful). Woodpeckers may be heard, buzzards have returned to the area and osprey have been seen on local lakes. There is much to enjoy and cherish here.

The walks outlined are of varying lengths along paths that have improved greatly in recent years, Most walks can be completed in half a day, but to enjoys the longer ones you will need to allow more time. There are short-cut options on some walks and the minimum time to allow for each walk is given at the beginning of each description. See below (Three ways to use this book) for other options. I first started work on this book in 1996, with the aim of creating a series of family walks which could also become a long distance walk. There are over 120 miles of paths described here, enabling walkers of all abilities to enjoy the Essex countryside. Each walk has a common start/finish point with the next walk to enable complete flexibility for the walker. The countryside is always changing with paths being diverted and stiles removed. When I first started work on this book many paths were difficult to follow, but thankfully this has changed. Where finding the route of the path has recently been difficult, I have tried to give a detailed description of the route; however, you may find this description superfluous as there has been a recent vast improvement in the state of the rights of way and the path could be well-defined.
Enjoy your walks!

Peter Cooper, 2011

Three Ways to use this Book

OPTION 1: Circular Walks - Each walk has a chapter of its own and you can start at either end of the walk, as the return route section is separated from the outward section. Where there are shorter walk options, these are described at the end of each section.

OPTION 2: Linear walks - Linear walks can be completed by just using either the outward or return sections of more than one walk. This may require two cars, parking one at the beginning and one at the end of the walk, or using public transport.

Examples: hourly weekday bus services link the following places (check times and stopping places before travelling):

> Widdington, Rickling Green (main road) and Stansted.
> Henham, Elsenham and Stansted
> Broxted, Thaxted and Debden.

Trains run daily linking Stansted, Elsenham and Great Chesterford.

OPTION 3: Long-distance linear walk - This may be done either way round, linking all the walks, and will take about three days each way.

Symbols used in sketch maps

POINT A, B, C	**Shortcut options**
1, 2, 3 etc	**Features of interest numbered with key**
- - - ➔ - - - -	**Paths used with direction of route**
- - - - - - - -	**Other paths**
=========	**Roads and lanes**
✝	**Church**
~~	**Rivers**

Further Information

Maps: Sketch maps are included with each walk, but these are intended to be only a basic guide, and not to scale. Walkers are <u>strongly</u> advised to buy the appropriate Ordnance Survey Explorer map(s): numbers 194, 195, 209, and 210 will be required for the whole route. The OS grid reference for the start point of each walk is given in the text.

Problems with footpaths, signposts etc. should **not** be reported to the author but to Essex Highways Department: telephone 0845 6063 7631 or via the Essex County Council website (follow the options to 'rights of way'). All the routes were walked during the winter of 2010/11 but as mentioned above are subject to variation.

Public Transport: tel: 0871 200 22 33 or <u>www.traveline.info</u> or text 84268.

Tourist Information for accommodation and other local help 01799 524002. Website <u>www.visitsaffronwalden.gov.uk</u> , or visit the individual village websites via <u>www.recordinguttlesfordhistory.org.uk</u> Ickleton near Great Chesterford also offers accommodation.

Facilities

Shops: At the time of writing there are shops open in Stansted, Clavering, Great Chesterford, Ashdon, Thaxted, Debden, Henham and Elsenham.

Pubs: At the time of writing there are pubs open near all the start points of the walks except Duddenhoe End, Strethall, Radwinter and Broxted (see text).

Please keep dogs on leads near livestock and crops which may have recently been sprayed. A full version of the Country Code can be found inside the back cover.

UPDATES TO THIS BOOK WILL BE PLACED FROM TIME TO TIME ON THE RECORDERS OF UTTLESFORD HISTORY WEBSITE, BY THEIR KIND PERMISSION: <u>www.recordinguttlesfordhistory.org.uk</u>

Acknowledgements

My thanks for help with this book to many people, but particularly to my wife Jacqueline for her expertise in assisting with the layout and editing, and her constant advice during the preparation of the book. Also to Carol Wilkinson, who interpreted my attempt at map-drawing and put them into legible form for publication. Lizzie Sanders and Gordon Ridgewell were very helpful with the cover design. Finally, to Norman and Barbara Rider, who bravely walked the routes, correcting errors and advising me when the instructions needed improvement.

List of Illustrations
Images © Peter & Jacqueline Cooper.

Cover photo: Uttlesford sign at Clavering; Title page: stile at Elmdon; Walks Photos: p.3 – Manuden church & Yew Tree pub; p.4 – Manuden Domesday plaque; p.5 - warning sign; p.6 – Stansted windmill; p.7 – Wellingtonia, Manuden; p.10 – Rickling Green cricket pavilion clock & windvane, road sign; p.11- duck house; p.15 – Rickling Church; p.16 – Hill Green, Clavering; p.17 – Trig Point, Clavering; p.20 – Clavering Mill; p.21 – Donkeys, Clavering; p.24 – Hamlet Church, Duddenhoe End; p.26 – stile, Elmdon; p.27 – Elmdon Dial stained glass; p.28 – Gravestone inscription, Strethall; p.29 – date on house, Strethall; p.31 – Strethall Church porch; p.33 – Great Chesterford village sign; p.34 – Icknield Way sign; p.35 – River Granta, Great Chesterford; p.38 – Waymarks & Len's Path sign, Hadstock; p.39 – Hadstock village green; p.44 – Ashdon village sign; p.45 – Ashdon Museum; p.47 – Hadstock Church; p.48 – Rose & Crown, Ashdon; p.52 – Radwinter School; p.53 – Radwinter Church porch; p.57 – Millennium Seat, Radwinter; p.61 – Giffords Farm chimney; p.62 – Radwinter village sign; p.63 – Thaxted windmill; p.68 – Guildhall, Thaxted; p.69 – Thaxted Church; p.70 – Debden village sign; p.73 – natural wood seat; p.74 – Widdington Church; p.75 – Widdington village sign; p.77 – fishing sign; p.78 – llama, Henham Lodge; p.80 – Widdington footpath sign & Henham village sign; p.81 – ducks, Henham pond; p.83 – candelabra, Chickney Church; p.84 – Hostage Window, Broxted Church; p.86 – school sign, Henham; p.89 - Crown Inn, Elsenham; p.90 – Robin Hood Road sign; p.92 – Elsenham Place; p.93 – pump shelter, Elsenham; p.87 – St Mary's Church, Stansted; p.98 – Stansted Hall; p.100 – Turners Spring nature reserve information board.

List of Walks

THE UTTLESFORD WAY

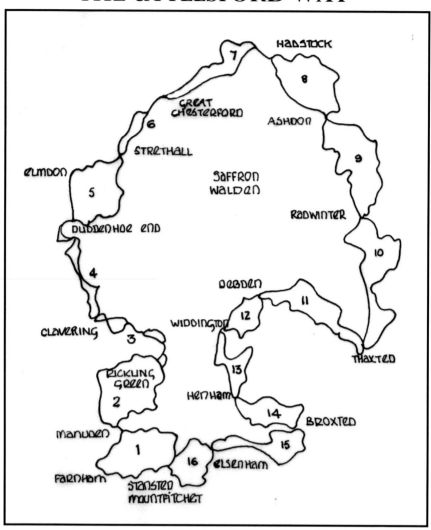

16 linked circular walks
See Contents list overleaf for key to numbers
See first page of each walk for start point OS ref.
Total distance for entire route: 127 miles

Walk One: 7½ miles   Start TL514248
Stansted Mountfitchet to Manuden

Stansted Mountfitchet is a large village served by trains operating between London and Cambridge, and good local weekday bus services linking Bishop's Stortford to Saffron Walden. Stansted Airport and local villages. There are shops, cafes and pubs. Accommodation is also available. Among the local attractions are a castle, toy museum and a windmill. Pay car parking is available at the station and opposite the castle. Street parking on the main roads in the village is restricted. The walk starts at the Station entrance and will take a minimum of 3 hours to complete the 7½ mile circular walk (3¼ miles out and 4¼ miles back). There are no shops along the route but there are pubs at Manuden and Hazel End – both serve food. Most of the route is on good footpaths, but there is some road walking along quiet lanes after leaving Stansted and into Hazel End. Manuden is poorly served by buses and the only link to Stansted Mountfitchet is in the early morning. The link point if continuing on to Rickling Green is the *Yew Tree* pub. Stansted is a Saxon word meaning 'stoney place' and Mountfitchet is derived from the Monfitchet family who took over the Manor from the Gernon family after the Norman Conquest, and later founded an Augustinian Priory at Thremhall which was dissolved by Henry VIII.

At the Station **[1]** you leave through the exit on the Cambridge-bound platform side and go straight down the road, passing some take-away restaurants, to the *Kings Arms* pub. Cross the busy road and continue in the same direction, passing the *Queens Head* pub and some small shops towards the traffic lights. Keep to the left at the lights along Lower Street, and cross the road before the *Dog & Duck* pub so that you fork **right** to stay on Lower Street. At the youth centre, continue straight ahead into Gaul End. Here the road becomes narrower with trees growing on the embankment to the right. Keep to the left of North End House and go through the gate with the ditch to your left. Soon you reach a field on your right – follow the path and at the corner of the field, turn **right** and continue up for about 50 yards. Turn **left** through the hedge and follow the well-trodden path under trees and beside a small coniferous plantation to Alsa Lane. Some of the land to your right, including the woods, forms part of the Aubrey Buxton Nature Reserve **[2]** which is administered by the Essex Wildlife Trust.

1

Walk 1: Stansted Mountfitchet to Manuden

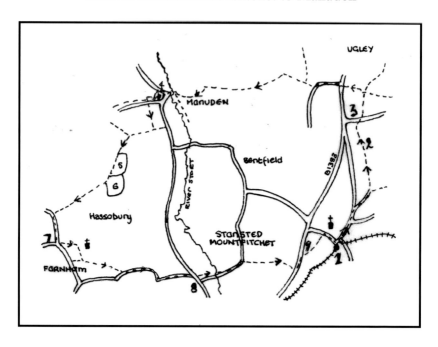

1. **Stansted Mountfitchet Station – START & FINISH**
2. **Nature Reserve**
3. **Rifle Range**
4. **Yew Tree pub – LINK POINT FOR RICKLING**
5. **Oozes Wood**
6. **Home Wood**
7. **Farnham School**
8. ***Three Horseshoes* pub, Hazel End**
9. **Stansted Windmill**

Turn **right** along the lane, and opposite the boundary fence of the weather-boarded buildings, take a footpath on the **left**. Follow this path into the woods where there are signs advising a rifle-range **[3]** to your left. Stay on the path until after you reach a gate. Keep the hedge on your right to the end of this field, where there is a tree with painted arrows on it – here, you turn **left** down to the main road. The big house on the right is occupied by the Home Farm Trust.

Walk 1: Stansted Mountfitchet to Manuden

Prior to the M11 being built, this was the A11 and the main route between London and Norwich. This stretch of road, now the B1383, carries a lot of traffic between Saffron Walden and Bishop's Stortford, hence care is needed when crossing the road to join the very small lane opposite, known as Pennington Lane. On this corner there used to be a stone marking the boundary between Stansted and Ugley, but it has recently disappeared from the grass at the junction.

Stay on Pennington Lane and go round the left-hand bend. Just before the next hedge, but before reaching the caravan, turn **right** onto a signposted bridleway at a green gate. Follow this track for about 75 yards until it reaches a junction with a second bridleway - here, you take the **left-hand** track and climb gently towards open countryside with views across fields. You are now over 300 feet above sea level, which is high for Essex. Stay on the bridleway as it slowly descends, crossing a farm-track, then over a ditch. Just before reaching a small wood, turn **left** and follow the woodland edge for a short distance until the next corner. Here you go through the hedge and walk down the field, keeping this hedge on your left. At the bottom of the field, turn **left** behind a house to a gate and then go down a steep grassy bank. There may be sheep here these days but once, in 1789, you would have encountered a different atmosphere on this hill, when crowds gathered to witness Richard Savill being hung for the murder of Thomas Bray, following a drunken fight while returning from Stansted.

At the track, turn **right** to go through a gate. Until destroyed by fire in 1888, Manuden Hall stood on the slope to the right of this gate. Turn **left** over the River Stort into Manuden, with the *Yew Tree* inn **[4]** on the corner. The village was known as *Magghedana* at one time and changed the spelling of its name several times over the centuries before settling on its current form. The parish covers about 2,500 acres but is thinly populated - according to the 1981 census there were then

3

only 616 people, down from 752 in 1861. The *Yew Tree* is the link point for the walk to Rickling Green which is described in the next chapter. To return to Stansted, read on. If you choose to continue to Rickling Green there is a direct weekday bus service along the main road back to Stansted Mountfichet.

RETURN ROUTE TO STANSTED

Manuden Parish Church is opposite the pub, and there is a gate on the right-hand corner of the churchyard near the Domesday plaque - follow the path, keeping the church to your left until you meet another path. Here you turn **right**, climbing beside the churchyard extension up to a gate, where you turn **left** down to the lane.

Cross the lane and climb the steps to the right of 'Top Cottage' onto a field-edge path, keeping beside a garden and allotments until it becomes a cross-field path, from which you will see some farm buildings and machinery ahead to your left. When you reach the track leading to the farm, turn **right** away from the buildings to the top of the field.

At the top, turn **left** staying in the same field along a wide track, keeping the bushes to your right. The footpath then turns **right** to cross the centre of a field following the line of the telegraph wires. When the path reaches the corner of Oozes Wood **[5]**, walk to the right of the woodland, which becomes Home Wood **[6]** when the path turns slightly to the right.

The buildings you can see through the trees used to form part of the Hassobury Estate which, according to the Domesday survey, was held in 1086 by a free man. It then passed to the Gernon and Montfichet families as an extension to their Stansted estates. In 1773 the estate became part of the Gosling family holdings and, when the mansion was rebuilt in 1868, some 17th century coins were discovered. It then became Waterside School for part of the 20th century, but the prep school closed during the 1980s. I would think those buildings bearing names such as Elms and Ash, now private houses, were once the dormitories.

As the woodland peters out, keep going to the end of the field, and then slip **left** down into a wooded glade and follow the (potentially muddy) bridleway. Go over Bourne Brook, then through a gate to cross two meadows towards the left-hand corner of Savenend Farm yard,

Walk 1: Stansted Mountfitchet to Manuden

before following a track to the lane. Turn **left** along the lane and pass Farnham School **[7]**, which shares its head teacher with the small village school at Rickling. The Gosling family of Hassobury were very generous to the village and set up a trust in 1909 to enable the village school children to take part in the annual Gosling feast - enjoying roast beef, turkey, roast potatoes and vegetables, followed by apple crumble and custard!

Other than the village hall and playing fields, Farnham being a small place on the very edge of Essex, has no facilities for the visitor. Turn **left** again, down the track to Farnham Church (which is likely to be locked). The church was rebuilt in 1859, again by the Gosling family, but very little is known about the previous building. Just before you reach the church, turn **right** onto the open fields and, before reaching the hedge, go **left** across the field, passing a lone tree on your left. Walk to the corner of the field, and through a gap to a bridge over Bourne Brook and a tiny lane.

You will have no problems here because you turn **left** onto the lane and up the hill towards some cottages on a double bend, and on to Hazel End. At the bend you may see the spire of St Michael's Church in Bishop's Stortford and hear the traffic on the town's by-pass. As you approach Hazel End, you may notice this interesting sign.

At the junction, the *Three Horseshoes* pub **[8]** is a few yards along to the right. It was near here in 1891 that a Neolithic greenstone axehead was found. Our route continues across the cricket field along the footpath immediately opposite the junction. If a match is in progress, go round the field to a line of trees to the right of the paddocks and keep the trees to your left all the way down to the lane. This quiet lane links Hazel End to Bentfield Green. Turn **left** onto the lane and cross the River Stort. Immediately after passing the drive of Watermill Farm, turn **right** up the footpath to cross the field and head for the single telegraph pole close to Limekiln Lane. Cross over the lane and continue uphill, keeping the hedge to your right as the buildings of Stansted Mountfitchet begin to come into view.

5

Walk 1: Stansted Mountfitchet to Manuden

The path feels claustrophobic, as it runs between two high fences before coming out on the main road. Looking right here, you may notice *The Bell* public house. This is a former coaching inn, a very busy place once with four or five coaches a day calling in to change horses on their way between London and Cambridge. In addition to this, there was a twice-weekly carrier's cart.

Turn **left** up the road and cross it, using the traffic island at the village sign depicting Magna Carta, welcoming you to the village. Climb up Mill Hill on your **right** to the recently restored Stansted Windmill **[9]**, which is open during summer afternoons on the first Sunday of each month and Bank Holiday Mondays. The windmill was built on land granted a 2000-year lease in 1580. In 1787 Joseph Lindsell built a windmill, malthouse and villa. The villa later became the Roman

Catholic Church, before a new church was built at the northern edge of the village. The malt house, though, was destroyed by fire in 1877 and the mill stopped working in 1910. In 1941 it was used as a Scout hut and 11 years later Scheduled as an Ancient Monument. In 1966 it was opened to the public.

Turn **left** beside the mill and stay on the road, keeping left on to Millside, which then changes its name to Woodfields, coming out opposite what is now Stansted Free Church. Turn **right** down the hill, passing the Skuba Diving Centre, and so back to the car park and station.

Walk Two: 8½ miles

Start TL492266

Manuden to Rickling Green

Manuden is a small, attractive village with no shop but there is a pub, the *Yew Tree* which is opposite the church and is the starting point for the walk. There is no off-street parking and the best place to park a car is on the main road opposite Manuden House, but not too near the bend. It will take a minimum of 3½ hours to complete the 8¾ mile circular walk (3½ miles out and 5¼ miles back). There are no shops along the route, but the *Cricketers Arms* at Rickling Green has recently re-opened. The route out is on good paths, and the way back includes some cross-field paths and road walking. There is no direct bus link but an hourly weekday service operates on the main road and will take you back to Stansted Mountfitchet. The link point, if continuing on to Clavering, is the cricket pavilion beside the green.

From the *Yew Tree* at Manuden [1], turn **right** with the church on your left. As you walk along the main road known as The Street, you will pass several listed buildings, and also some large Wellingtonia trees in the grounds of Manuden House. In 1989/90 the house featured in Marjorie Allingham's detective series with Peter Davison playing Campion. Other buildings of note include the one next to the pub, formerly a bakery, the old maltings where you can still see the grain hoist, and an old shop where, in 1900, the proprietor was also the undertaker. Cleeve Hall was one of several building in the village that served as a vicarage, Cobbs was the Congregational Chapel until 1956 and Wren Cottage, on the corner of Mailers Lane, was the home of Revd Thomas Bayley, who was burnt at the stake at Smithfield in 1431 for heresy.

After the bend, there is a large meadow on the right, where cattle may be seen. Immediately after passing the village hall, you will notice Wagoners Court on the left - this used to be a pub, and next door was a slaughter house. Just after house no.74, take the footpath on your **right**, and walk between the houses and beside a huge tree - the route then opens out into the fields, where you continue in the same direction to a footbridge over the River Stort.

7

Walk 2: Manuden to Rickling Green

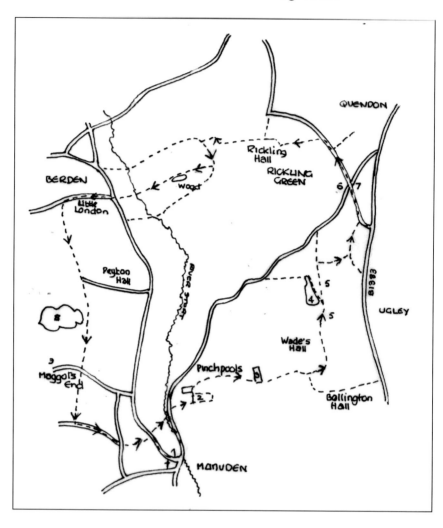

1. The *Yew Tree* pub –
   START & FINISH
2. The Hall Wood
3. Wakeling's Wood
4. Burney Wood
5. Broom Wood

6. Cricket Pavilion – LINK
   POINT FOR
   CLAVERING
7. The *Cricketers Arms*
8. Battles Wood
9. Battles

Walk 2: Manuden to Rickling Green

Turn **left** over the stile into a meadow between the river and a lane. Leave the meadow at the next stile and cross the lane to climb the path up towards The Hall Wood **[2]**. On reaching the wood, turn **left** beside it and at the far end drop down to the corner of Crouch Hill Wood, which you then keep to your left until you cross the footbridge and turn **right** up the track.

The views behind are well worth turning round for, and in the valley you may notice the farm buildings at Pinchpools, one of the original four manors of Manuden. The Stort Valley opens up, and the Pelham Grid station can be seen in the distance. The small wood on the left has a pond inhabited by Mallard ducks.

After passing the wood, the path turns a little to the **right** and as it leads up to Wakeling's Wood **[3]**, where you may spot cowslips in the ditch. Many of the small woods in the area are maintained for breeding pheasants, so stick to the paths and keep dogs on leads. Once you have passed the wood, the view in front changes. Traffic can be seen going through Ugley on the B1383, and beyond that the netting of the refuge tip is visible.

Nearer at hand are the farm buildings of Bollington Hall. Go down the hill to the larger track and turn **right** into the farmyard, and then **left** between the barns and shelters where several pieces of machinery are kept. At the end of the buildings, cross the grass strip and turn **left** onto the farm drive and to Wades Hall. This site has recently been completely redeveloped and the former dilapidated barns, which must have been a haven for wildlife, are no more.

Stay on the track to Broom Wood, which commences on the right, where there is a tree planted in memory of Cecil and Lily Prior who died in the late 1990s. Just before the point where trees appear on the left, turn **left** and soon you will enter the partly coniferous Burney Wood **[4]**. When the path turns to the **left**, there is a pond to the right (assuming it has water), and after passing this pond, turn **right** over the ditch onto a wide cross-field path.

Follow the path to the first hedge, and turn **right** up to the edge of Broom Wood **[5]** again. In May, bluebells can be seen in this wood but they are not as spectacular as in Coney Acre, the other side of Rickling Green.

Turn **left** at the wood and stay beside it until you reach the lane where you turn **left** into the village and the large green with its cricket pavilion, unusual clock and cricket-themed windvane **[6]**.

Walk 2: Manuden to Rickling Green

Rickling Green has a pub, the *Cricketers Arms* [7] on the opposite side of the green to the pavilion. It did once have a part-time post office, but that finally closed in 2008. (If on leaving the wood, you turn right, there is a weekday hourly bus service linking Bishop's Stortford and Saffron Walden along the main road. You would need to cross the road to catch the bus for Stansted Mountfitchet and Bishop's Stortford.) The cricket pavilion is the link point of the next stage of the walk, which is described in the next chapter. To return to Manuden, read on.

RETURN ROUTE TO MANUDEN

At the junction by the cricket pavilion **[6]**, where there is a signpost telling how far it is to almost everywhere, follow Brick Kiln Lane towards Rickling Church and Wicken Bonhunt. Leave the village and, if it is bluebell time, go up the bridleway beside Redlands to look at the display in Coney Acre. Otherwise, stay on the lane, passing another wood on the left down to a pond and some white railings. Turn **left** here keeping the hedge to your right up to Rickling Hall,

10

Walk 2: Manuden to Rickling Green

where you go between some farm buildings, before turning **right** and then **left** on the concrete drive, passing a pond with an elaborate duck house and the arch to the courtyard of Rickling Hall on your left. Stay on the drive and, immediately after passing a large tree on each side of the drive, turn **left** before reaching the fencing, keeping a paddock on your left, and follow the track into open countryside.

On reaching a waymark at the end of the trees, leave the track where it turns right and continue in the same direction across the field, aiming to the left of two small trees where there is a footbridge over the ditch. You will notice a damaged, partly concrete footpath sign which indicated that you turn **right** beside the hedge to a similar post about 200 yards along the field edge - there is also a tree in the hedge here. Turn **left** and walk across the field to the hedge and another concrete signpost (which may be hidden by foliage) - here you turn **left** down to the corner of the same field.

Go into the next field and turn **right** here along the field-edge to the next corner, where you cross the plank bridge. Turn **right** then **left** round the edge of the next field until you reach the next bridge on your right just before the wood. Cross the bridge and, keeping the trees to your left, enjoy the view as you descend to a bridge over the River Stort. There are often sheep in the fields to your left. Cross the bridge and follow the hedged path to the right - this path is easy to find but can be difficult underfoot, so take care.

Walk up to the Clavering-Manuden road, which you cross onto the lane leading to Little London, a tiny hamlet in the parish of Berden, consisting of a collection of cottages and houses along the road and a couple of small lanes. The community supported its own pub long after the last pub closed in the main village. When you reach a weather-boarded barn at Petley House Farm near the letter-box, turn **left** along the track past Jersey Farm towards Rowan Cottage, where you join the grass track which becomes a field-edge path.

Walk 2: Manuden to Rickling Green

Keep the hedge to your left as the path winds a little, and just before the meadow, opposite a footpath you may notice a Friendship Oak planted in 1998 on the parish boundary between Berden and Manuden. Continue to the beginning of the second meadow, and go through the gate on your **left** to walk diagonally in front of Peyton Hall to the gate at the far corner. There may be farm animals in this field, and from time to time there is a sign advising that it is occupied by a bull.

Leave the field and turn **right** along the track beside a house. At the footpath sign. where the track turns left, carry straight on keeping the ditch to your right, then go through a gap in the hedge. Enter the field and keep the hedge to your left as you head towards Battles Wood **[8]**. During the Middle Ages, Battles Hall **[9]** (which is not on our route), was probably the most important residence in the area. It was also the site of a murder in 1677. The manor was awarded to Humphry Bataille after the Norman Conquest and stayed in the family until 1401. In 1574, three-year-old Ann Walker inherited the estate, and, when she was only 15, married William Waad, who later reputedly became the first Englishman to discover America. He was knighted in 1603, became an MP and was allegedly responsible for eliciting a signature on Guy Fawkes' confession after torturing him on the rack.

Follow the direction of the waymark across the next field (if the path is not re-instated, turn right and head for the edge and walk beside the wood). At the far corner go over the ditch near a large tree. Cross the next field by walking in the same direction as in the previous field, towards the houses and as you get nearer to these, your route between them becomes clearer, although the path across this field is not always as clear as it should be. Once you can see the fence, you will also see the route between two paddocks to the left of the pink house, which leads out onto the drive of Maggots End Farm. Follow the drive out to the lane, which you cross then climb up to the path opposite to walk beside some more paddocks. Follow the line of telegraph poles to the next field, where you follow the hedge to the back-garden boundary of a house - here, you go down the bank and follow the fence to the road, where you turn **left** towards the west end of Manuden.

At the next junction, turn **right** and after a few yards, turn **left** down Butt Lane, which brings you to the main road through the village. Turn **right** towards the *Yew Tree* pub.

Walk Three: 7½ miles   Start TL511298
Rickling Green to Clavering

We start this walk beside the oldest cricket ground in Essex, at Rickling Green. The pavilion is very modern and provides a challenge to the batsman before they even get to the wicket, inasmuch as they have to cross the road. Once a year, usually as part of the benefit programme of the county beneficiary, several Essex and ex-England players take part in a six-a-side tournament at this ground. On that occasion it is not the peaceful village green that it is the rest of the year. The walk begins at the cricket pavilion and will take at least 2¾ hours to complete the 7½ miles (3¾ miles each way). This is a figure-of-eight walk, with the stretch between Rickling Church and Moat Farm being walked in both directions. This also gives an option for two shorter circular walks to Rickling Church and back. There are 2 pubs and a shop in Clavering, but the village is poorly served by buses. Most of the walk is on good paths and tracks, with the longest stretch of road walking being on a pavement in Clavering. The link point to continue on to Duddenhoe End is the thatched cricket pavilion in Clavering.

From the pavilion cross the road and walk on the left of the green in the direction of the *Cricketers Arms* [1], passing the tiny school on your right. Although the school is small, it is popular and attracts students from surrounding villages. The former village hall is also on your right before you turn **left** along Woodside. Rickling and Quendon are very closely associated, and both have churches and share the same vicar with Berden and Manuden. Rickling Green is the main population centre, and is more associated with Quendon, which also boasts of a famous son in William Winstanley, builder of the Eddystone Lighthouse.

The bridleway soon enters Coney Acre [2], one of several important woods in the area - one of them, Quendon Wood, is an SSSI. This wood is a mass of blue in May when the bluebells are in flower. These are also the last woods that we actually walk through for some time. In the winter, finches, tits and wrens may be spotted flitting between trees, and deer from the nearby Quendon Estate can often be seen. At the waymark post, keep **right** and follow the footpath along the boundary of Quendon House. At the end of the garden, turn **left** and after about 10 yards, take the path on the **right** to the end of the woods, where you leave through a gap in the bushes.

13

Walk 3: Rickling Green to Clavering

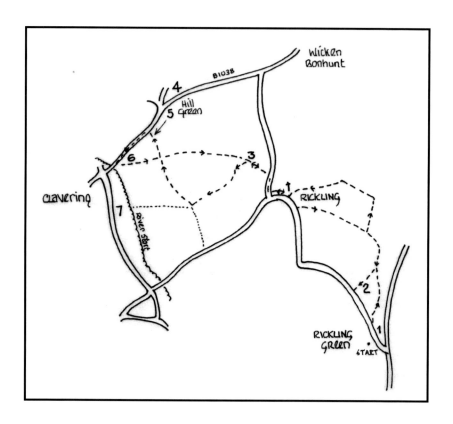

Cricket Pavilion – START & FINISH

1 - *Cricketers Arms*, Rickling Green
2 - Coney Acre
3 - Moat Farm
4 - *Cricketers* pub, Clavering
5 - Clavering cricket pavilion – LINK POINT FOR DUDDENHOE END
6 - *Fox & Hounds* pub, Clavering
7 - Clavering village supermarket

Walk 3: Rickling Green to Clavering

Continue straight ahead across the field along an established footpath to a signpost in the hedge opposite. Then turn **left**, keeping the hedge on your left down to the track, where you turn **right** down and up the hill, keeping to the right at the top so that you remain beside the trees.

After about ½ mile, at the top of a hill and immediately after a hedge, turn **left** along the track towards a gate, where you keep left towards some farm buildings. Pass a thatched cottage on the right and a converted barn on the left, before reaching the lane at Rickling Church. Turn **right** through the churchyard, which in the spring is a carpet of daffodils. Keep the church to your right as you aim for the stile in the left-hand corner.

After climbing over a second stile, keep to the left of the field as you make your way up to the lane, where you turn **right**. Go through a large gap in the hedge about 200 yards on the **left**, where you cross the field to a bridge beside a wet-weather pond in the right-hand corner. Stay in the same direction through the meadow until you reach another bridge, then walk beside another pond to a gap on the **right**. Go through the gap, and immediately **left**, keeping the house to your right.

This house, once known as Moat Farm **[3]**, was notorious at the beginning of the 20th century, when the owner was hanged at Chelmsford for a murder committed here. Over a hundred years after such notoriety, it is very quiet here now.

15

Walk 3: Rickling Green to Clavering

Continue up the hedged track to the top, and turn **left** on the wide field-edge path. There is an old pond on the left, before the path turns **right** - this is Gypsy Lane and is believed to be the old road to Rickling. It is now an attractive hedged path, but liable to be muddy at times as it gradually descends. Almost opposite a byway on your left, known as Highfield Lane, you need to turn **right** to follow a cross-field path diagonally left, aiming for the corner of a hedge. From this point, cross into the next field and from this height you can see the Stocking Pelham grid station in the distance. Cross over a grass track (which leads down to Clavering village), and continue down to walk past a fence and over a footbridge. This track brings you out on Hill Green, where there is a thatched cricket pavilion **[5]** - formerly a WW2 airfield hut - a former Methodist chapel and an unusual wheeled pump.

Clavering has a well-stocked shop, but it is at the other end of the village in Stortford Road **[7]**. There are also two pubs, one of which is the *Cricketers* **[4]**, where a young Jamie Oliver cut carrots for his father – this is a couple of hundred yards to your right along the road. We will pass the other pub, the *Fox & Hounds* **[6]** on the way back. The link point if continuing on to Duddenhoe End is the thatched cricket pavilion.

RETURN ROUTE TO RICKLING GREEN

From the cricket pavilion **[5]**, walk towards the road and turn **left** past a pond and Whyman's plant nursery towards the *Fox & Hounds* **[6]**, reputed to be one of the oldest pubs in Essex. (To visit the village supermarket, stay on the High Street over the Bridges, where Kings Water joins the River Stort, up the hill and left at the junction - the shop **[7]** is at the end of the village.) Otherwise, after passing the

16

Walk 3: Rickling Green to Clavering

pub, turn **left** through its car park and walk up through the remnants of Town Meadow, where fairs were held in earlier times. Go through a gap at the top of the meadow onto the footpath and climb between the fields, as views of the village open up behind you. You will pass a point where you crossed over this path earlier. Stay on the path through a couple of fields until you reach a Trig Point almost hidden in the bushes. Here, at certain times of the year, you can see the radar station on the Saffron Walden to Debden road and, if it is clear enough, the tower of Newport Church.

At the Trig Point, go through into the next field, keeping the hedge on your left as you walk down towards some polytunnels - here turn **right** to the hedge, and follow it beside a garden onto a good path. You are now back at Moat Farm **[3]** and will be retracing your steps back to Rickling Church. Turn **left** to stay beside the garden, then **right** through a wide gap in the hedge, before turning **left** beside a pond and over a plank bridge into the next field. Now cross the field towards the right of some trees at a pond, then into the next field, where you aim for the gap in the hedge at the road. Turn **right** along the lane, then **left** besides the garden hedge and stone wall of 'The Old Vicarage'. Go over two stiles into the churchyard, and out onto the road.

At the little green outside the churchyard, turn **right** along the lane besides the letter box and, after a couple of cottages and a field, leave the road by taking the path on your **left** beside the hedge. On reaching the end of the field, continue through a gap in the hedge and cross the next field. When it reaches the track you came up earlier, go down the avenue of trees and bear **right** to follow the track and you will pass Coney Acre Wood **[2]** on your left before reaching the road. Turn **left** along the lane back to Rickling Green. In May you might like to divert into the woods just before the lane to see the dazzling display of flowers.

17

Walk Four: 9 miles
Clavering to Duddenhoe End

Start TL483326

Clavering is one of the larger villages in NW Essex, with a population of about 1,200 spread across nearly 4,000 acres There is scattered housing for nearly two miles along the B1368 Buntingford to Newport road, with the shop (in Stortford Road) and the church to the west of the village, the *Fox & Hounds* public house more central and the *Cricketers* [1], village hall and playing field nearer the eastern end of the village. The walk starts at the cricket pavilion opposite the village hall, and the full walk will take a minimum of 3½ hours to complete the 9 miles (4½ miles each way). This is a figure-of-eight walk with the cross-over on the Roman Road, where about 45 minutes can be saved if you decide not to visit Duddenhoe End. There is also a short-cut option near Clavering Farm described at the end of the walk, and this would cut the walk by half. There are no shops or pubs in Duddenhoe End, but there is a café at Clavering Lakes just off-route. The walk is mostly on good paths and tracks with the only road walking in the Duddenhoe End area. Both villages are linked by a shoppers' bus, but you are advised to check the timing if you plan to use it. The link point to continue onto Strethall is Duddenhoe End Village Hall.

From the cricket pavilion [2] head for the road, and go **left** until you reach a pond. Directly opposite is a footpath to the Jubilee Field. Keep to the left of the field to the corner, where you will find a slope with some steps down to a footbridge over Kings Water stream. Go through the little woodland and into a field, which you climb following the line of telegraph poles to a byway known locally as Coley Lane.

1. *The Cricketers* pub, Clavering
2. Clavering Cricket pavilion – START & FINISH
3. Wood Hall
4. Stocking Grove
5. Little Fosters
6. Godwells Grove
7. Duddenhoe End Village Hall – LINK POINT
8. Ford
9. Clavering Lakes cafe
10. *Fox & Hounds* pub; 11. Clavering supermarket

18

Walk 4: Clavering to Duddenhoe End

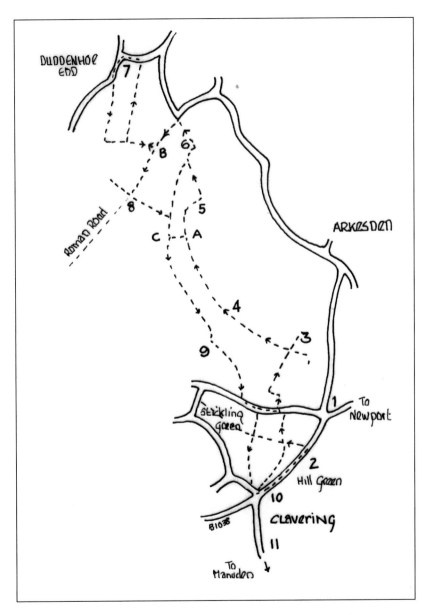

A, B & C – SHORTER WALK OPTIONS (see key opposite)

Walk 4: Clavering to Duddenhoe End

On the horizon ahead you may spot two windmills that no longer have their sails – these are privately-owned, but there are windmills at Stansted Mountfitchet, Ashdon and Thaxted that are open to the public on specific days, Thaxted being the most accessible. There used to be a third mill at Clavering, but it was blown down long ago.

At the byway, turn **right** down to Stickling Green Road. Turn **left** for about 200 yards until you reach a stile on the **right**, beside a gate leading into a meadow. Enter the meadow and keep to the edge beside some gardens, to the top left-hand corner where there is another stile to cross. The route goes beside a very long garden in which you may notice donkeys and sheep. Stay beside the hedge along to a track, which leads to a woodland near Wood Hall **[3]**, where daffodils abound in the spring. Upon reaching a junction of paths at the wood, **turn left** along the headland, with views over Kings Water and towards the Mills. The woods here support a variety of spring flowers, including numerous cowslips which also grow along the path. It is not unusual to see deer in this area, as there is a herd in Scotts Wood on the other side of the valley.

Walk 4: Clavering to Duddenhoe End

Stay along the top of the fields until you go through a gap in the hedge at the far end of Stocking Grove **[4]** – here, the temptation is to turn right, but in fact you need to turn **left** for a few yards and *then* turn **right** after the next hedge, and continue to walk above the valley where you can see the fishing lakes on the other side of Kings Water. Where the hedge turns right **(Point A)** just after a telegraph pole, turn **right** staying beside the hedge to the next corner where you continue in the same field by turning **left**. You are now 400 feet above sea level and have an opportunity to enjoy views over towards Arkesden and Saffron Walden.

At the next corner, slip though a gap in the hedge onto a track, where you turn **right**, passing the front of Little Fosters **[5]**. This track can get a little muddy at times, but stay on it until you join a road. Take the first track on the **left** up to remote Bulls Green Cottage. Here, an ancient hedgerow borders the track, varying season by season from brightly-coloured flowers to a rich abundance of fruit.

Walk 4: Clavering to Duddenhoe End

The track turns **right** near the cottage leading to Godwell's Grove **[6]** on your left. This is a lovely peaceful wood with signs of coppicing. Where the footpath crosses the track at the waymark signs, turn **left** into the woods and walk through to the other side. Leave it over a footbridge into a field, where you turn **right**, then **left** at the corner, staying in this field up to the Roman Road. The Roman Road at Coopers End today passes some industrial units, but 2,000 years ago it was part of a major route between the important Roman towns at Great Chesterford and Braughing. Turn **left** along the road until you turn **right** along the byway called Lorkins Lane **(Point B)**. A couple of hundred yards along Lorkings Lane, there is a footpath across the fields on the **right**. Cross the footbridge and walk over three fields divided by ditches and bridges, up to the edge of a paddock where once again there is a footbridge.

Once you reach the hedge, cross the bridge into a paddock and keep to the left edge beside the fence, up to a stile and track between houses to Duddenhoe End. There is a sign saying 'Brooksies' - here you turn **left** to the village hall **[7]**. Unfortunately there are no facilities at the village other than the hall and church. The pub closed a few years ago, but there is an interesting little selection of houses and cottages. Whilst there is a bus that links the hamlet with Clavering, it operates early in the morning. The link point if continuing on to Strethall is the village hall.

RETURN ROUTE TO CLAVERING

To return to Clavering, turn **left** along the road to the village hall, then **left** again, passing Duddenhoe End Farm. Where the road turns sharply to the right, carry straight on up the track towards White Friars Farm. About halfway up the drive, follow the waymark arrow on a telegraph pole pointing into the adjoining field on your **right**. Stay in the same direction as you head for the left-hand corner of the wood ahead of you, and then across the field to Lorkings Lane, where you turn **left** back towards the Roman Road **(Point B)**. Turn **right** onto the Roman Road, known as Beards Lane. Make sure that you keep **left** where the surfaced road turns right to Cosh Farm, and stay on the Roman Road until it dips down to a ford **[8]**, which may very well be dry. Here, you need to turn **left** through the hedge to follow the footpath. Keep the hedge to your right as you follow the path to the end of the field, where there is a path to Little Fosters on

Walk 4: Clavering to Duddenhoe End

your left. Ignore this path and continue along the sunken glade to the end, then climb the steep steps **(Point C)** on your **left**, before turning **right** again to follow the field edge path beside Kings Water for about a mile to the road at Stickling Green. On the other side of the stream, you will notice agricultural buildings at Clavering Farm, then some fishing lakes. If you wish to visit the café at the lakes **[9]**, there is a bridge on the right just before a field-edge hedge, and the café is the other side of the lakes to your right (it closes at 5 pm in the summer and 4 pm in the winter and does not open on a Monday). This bridge is *not* a right-of-way so can only be used by café customers. Retrace your steps back to Kings Water.

Before you reach the road, you will pass another fishing lake containing trout and will observe Clavering Place Farm, formerly the sub-manor of Geddings. At the road turn **left**, passing some large houses until you reach Stickling Green. Halfway along the green is a footpath sign on the **right**. Follow this to go between houses before crossing a footbridge. Climb between two fields following the line of electricity poles to the top, where there are good views to enjoy before dropping down towards the village of Clavering, over two stiles to the road beside Middle Street ford. In the grounds of Chestnut Cottage is a building said to be the smallest house in Essex. Cross the bridge and walk up Middle Street past pretty cottages, round the bend to a bus shelter, village information board and seat for a well-earned rest.

To continue to Rickling, turn **left** to the *Fox and Hounds* **[10]**, and for the cricket pavilion walk past the pub and stay on the road for a further half-mile. If you wish to visit the shop **[11]**, cross the road opposite the bus shelter, and go along Stortford Road past the school to the end of the village (normal closing time 5.30 pm or noon on Sundays).

SHORT CUTS
1.To halve the length of the walk, at **Point A** turn **left** and go down the cross-field path to the hedge, where you turn **left** again to pick up the walk at **Point C**. If walking from Duddenhoe End, after climbing the steps at **Point C**, the cross-field path starts slightly to your left. Once you have crossed the field to **Point A**, follow the field edge with the hedge on your right.
2.To cut about 45 minutes from the walk and not visit Duddenhoe End at **Point B**, move on in the text to **Point B** on the return route.

23

Walk Five: 7¾ miles   Start TL459366
Duddenhoe End to Strethall

Duddenhoe End is little more than a hamlet, even though it is the largest population centre in the parish of Wenden Lofts. It does have a village hall at the western end of the main street, where there is a sign that advises that you may park there if you are walking the local paths or 'brambling'. It is wise to ensure no events are taking place at the hall, or your vehicle could get blocked in. Public transport only just exists but its times may not be convenient. The walk starts at the village hall and will take a minimum of 3 hours to complete the 7¾ miles (3¾ miles out and 4 miles back). There are no shops or pubs en route, but the *Elmdon Dial* pub is less than half-a-mile off the route in the centre of Elmdon village. Most of the walk is on good paths and tracks, but one of the stiles is higher than average. It is also prone to being very muddy in the Strethall area. Exercise care on the short stretch of road walking along the B1039. Strethall is tiny and has no public transport – however, there is a shorter walk option linking Elmdon directly to Littlebury Green, which will cut about an hour off the walk from Duddenhoe End. The link point, if continuing on to Great Chesterford, is Strethall Church.

Go to the front of Duddenhoe End village hall **[1]** and turn **right** along the main street. The house opposite used to be the *Woodman* pub, and a little further along the road you will pass 'The Old Post Office' on the

24

Walk 5: Duddenhoe End to Strethall

right. At Toppins Meadow, turn **left** along a grassy footpath, with a paddock on your left. Pass beneath an oak tree onto a cross-field path, which goes over two fields to a lane. As you cross these fields, you will notice a thatched church on your left. By taking a slight diversion, this can be reached from the road.

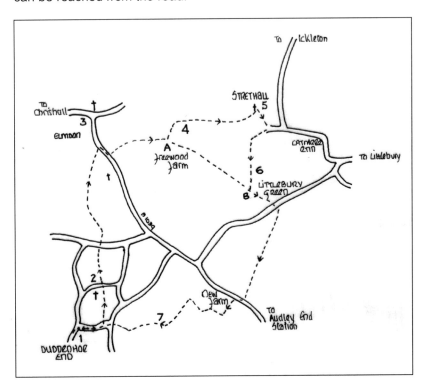

1. **Duddenhoe End Village Hall – START & FINISH**
2. **The Hamlet Church**
3. *Elmdon Dial* **pub**
4. **Free Wood**
5. **Strethall Church – LINK POINT FOR GT CHESTERFORD**
6. **Bixett Wood**
7. **Rockells Wood**

POINTS A & B – SHORTER WALK OPTIONS

25

Walk 5: Duddenhoe End to Strethall

The Hamlet Church **[2]** is a converted barn which was restored about 100 years ago at a cost of £25,000, a large sum for a small village before the days of English Heritage grants. Later on, the walk passes near to the disused church which was replaced by this one. This unusual building is well worth a visit and feels very welcoming. Not only was it not originally built as a church, it also appears to be in the garden of a private house, and the altar is at the centre of the long eastern wall of this former barn. The Hamlet Church shares its rector with six other churches, including Elmdon and Strethall.

From the footpath, cross the lane staying in the same direction, keeping on the path to the **right** of the hedge, down beside a line of horse chestnut trees, which are particularly striking in May when in blossom. Go down to the valley, where there is a little stream which winds its way to join the River Granta near Audley End. Your stay in the valley is only brief, as you turn **right** along the road for a few yards, before going **left** on another footpath over the stream and beside a newly-planted beech hedge on your left out of the valley. At the top, bear **left** where there are more signs of planting among the more mature bushes. Cross the track and keep the wood to your right. It can get a little muddy here.

This wood is one of several on this walk with a deep ditch round its edge, and is dominated by horse chestnut and elderberry. At the northern end of the wood, turn **right** over the bridge into the trees for a few yards and out to a high stile. Having negotiated the stile, walk between the fenced horse meadows up towards Elmdon sports field. On the right you will notice the tower of the old Wenden Lofts church in the grounds of Lofts Hall. This is private property, so the best view available is from the path. Lofts Hall was the former manor house of Wenden Lofts and, after being purchased by Sir Thomas Meade in 1567, was rebuilt and renamed Lofts Hall. The family lived there until 1717, when they sold the hall, along with much of Elmdon and Duddenhoe End, to a wealthy London merchant.

26

Walk 5: Duddenhoe End to Strethall

At the top of the path, go through the kissing-gate into the field used by Elmdon Cricket Club, which was formed in 1886, and the village football club. Keep on the right of the field noting the weeping willows beside the pond. At the road our route goes **right**, but to visit the pub, church and village green turn left. Elmdon is one of a small group of villages set on the chalky uplands of North Essex. The ridge is about 400 feet above sea level, and between here and Strethall you will enjoy occasional extensive views over the Cambridgeshire countryside. Elmdon has always been an agricultural village, with spinning and weaving also providing employment during the 18th and 19th centuries. In 1861 the village supported seven shepherds.

The bus shelter on the village green has performed an important function in the recent past which was nothing to do with public transport. The pub, in those days known as the *Kings Head*, was closed down against the wishes of the village. There was a long battle when the planning authorities received and rejected applications to convert it into a private house. Finally the property owner sold the property, which opened as licensed premises again in 2006. During the period of closure, a stalwart band of locals met twice a year for a drink at the bus shelter, which became known as the 'Kings Headless'! The pub is now called the *Elmdon Dial* **[3]**, a name taken from one of the windows in the parish church. Ironically, this is not a part of Elmdon's history, as the window was originally in Wenden Lofts Church and was moved after that church closed.

Back to the route: we had turned **right** after the playing field, and now pass several very nice houses towards the speed de-restriction sign. Before reaching this sign, turn **left** along the Icknield Way. This stretch is called Freewood Lane and takes us up to Freewood Farm, passing an ancient mill mound on the right, with a ditch round it. The Icknield Way is one of several long-distance trails maintained by Natural England, and links the Ridgeway Path at Ivinghoe Beacon to Pedders Way near Knettishall on the Suffolk / Norfolk border. The Icknield Way is unusual in that it provides a path for walkers, and also a route for horse-riders and cyclists – sometimes, but not always, they share the same route. Because of the route options, it is not true to the ancient route, and to

27

make it even more confusing, it is also called Ickleton Way in Berkshire. The Icknield Way is a relative newcomer as a long-distance trail, and makes it almost possible to walk from Sheringham in Norfolk to Lands End using only long-distance trails.

We will take advantage of this trail on this and the next two walks, before we turn back south and the trail heads north. At Freewood Farm **(Point A)**, where you may see some cows, pass the first farm building, then turn **left** at a waymark towards Free Wood **[4]**. Stay on the path to the left of the wood, noting that once again there is a ditch round it. This was probably dug a lot deeper in medieval times to keep out wild animals including deer – however, the remaining shallow ditch no longer keeps the deer out - signs of them are everywhere. Another sign that this is an ancient wood is the proliferation of bluebells. At the corner of the wood, turn **right** along the track, continuing to keep the trees on your right, with fine views over Cambridgeshire to your left. Remain on this track when Strethall Wood appears on the left. A view of Strethall can be seen through a gap in the trees.

You will have been on the path for some time before you reach a waymark sign. Turn **left** here along a path which goes down beside steep banks to a meadow. Follow the path down to the bottom where it turns **right** into a field, and in the middle of the field take the path on your **left,** up to Strethall Hall Farm and Strethall Church **[5]**. Go through the gate to the churchyard. Here, on a gravestone in memory of former Red Cross nurse, Janet Patience Cameron Adams MBE, is this verse:

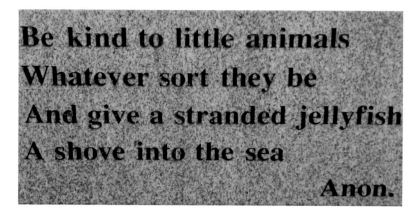

Be kind to little animals
Whatever sort they be
And give a stranded jellyfish
A shove into the sea

Anon.

The link point if continuing on to Great Chesterford is the Church.

28

RETURN ROUTE TO DUDDENHOE END

If you thought Duddenhoe End was small, Strethall is tiny. It consists of little more than a farm and a church. Catmere End, with its 20 or so houses up the road, now forms part of the parish, but it is still too small to support any services other than a school bus which picks up a couple of students for the schools at Great Chesterford and Saffron Walden. The tiny church, which can easily seat the whole population, is the focal point and well worth a visit and a few quiet moments. It wasn't so quiet one week in 1849 when a burglar was shot at Strethall Hall during a break-in. His body was placed in the church tower where the sexton charged threepence to view it. The story reached London and the lanes were blocked with carriages as the masses came to see this renowned criminal.

With your back to the church porch, turn **left** through the churchyard to the gate, and down a slope to join a footpath, which continues to descend before climbing gently beside an old barn and a couple of ponds to a lane on the outskirts of Catmere End. Turn **right** along the lane, passing Ryders, a thatched house with the date 1550 on the pargetted plaster. At Potash Cottage, leave the lane and take the track to the **left** of the cottage. This can be muddy at times, in which case it might be better to walk on the field-edge. At the end of the first field, take the hedged bridleway on the **left** down to an open field, where it may also be muddy. Continue on to pass Bixett Wood **[6]**, another ancient woodland, with ditches, bluebells and ponds. Keep the wood on your left, until the path swings right into a broad grass track. After about 200 yards, turn **left** at the waymark post **(Point B)**, following the bridleway until you reach the road at Littlebury Green. This small village has a Victorian church and plenty of nice houses, but all its pubs have long since closed.

29

Walk 5: Duddenhoe End to Strethall

Cross over the road and follow a track between a brick-barn conversion and a building with a cow weathervane on the roof. This little stretch can be full of life or completely dead - if there is water in the ponds, the ducks are likely to announce your appearance – where do they go once the ponds dry out? Cows and sheep can be seen in the fields, and further down the track rabbits will be scuttling for cover. At the hedge where the track turns left, you need to turn **right** along the top of the field. Admire the view over the valley, before turning **left** at the corner of that field, to drop 150 feet down to the valley bottom and a road. This is a B-road, so exercise caution. Turn **right** over a stream, and follow the road uphill to New Farm, where you turn **left** into the farmyard and continue beside the hedge, following the edge of a huge field as it turns right and left, until you are walking beside a long, thin piece of woodland to your left. At the gap in the trees, which is the corner of Rockells Wood **[7]**, turn **left** between the trees and up the slope, keeping the woods on your right, as first you climb then drop down to a hedge. On a clear day, you may be rewarded not only by the woodland flora, but also wide views to the east, as far as Saffron Walden and Debden.

Rockells Wood is another ancient woodland with wild flowers, but the ditches are less obvious and, like the other woods on this walk, it is private. It is a long pleasant walk beside the wood and you finally drop down to a hedge where there is a choice of routes but you need to go through the hedge and **diagonally** across the field ahead under a line of telegraph poles to a track. Turn **right** along the track to a road junction, which you cross and pass the houses back to the village hall.

SHORT CUT: At Freewood Farm **(Point A)**, do not turn left but continue straight on beside the farm buildings, and then to the right of the hedge, staying in a straight line until you reach **Point B**. If walking the shorter route from Strethall, turn right at **Point B** and keep the hedge to your right as you walk towards Free Wood and the farm buildings. Just before the last barn turn right up to Free Wood **(Point A).**

Walk Six: 5½ miles
Strethall to Great Chesterford

<u>Start TL485398</u>

There is a shortage of rights-of-way in this north-western corner of Essex, which means that much of this walk involves retracing your steps. If doing this walk on its own, it will be better to start at Great Chesterford when the walk becomes a 'frying-pan' walk (out on the handle, round the rim of the pan and back along the handle again). I will, however, start by describing the route from Strethall to follow on from the previous walk. The walk starts at Strethall Church and will take a minimum of 1¾ hours to walk the 5½ miles (2¾ miles each way) There is very limited parking at Strethall, but free parking in Great Chesterford where there are pubs and a shop, as well as buses and trains, However there is no direct public transport link with Strethall. Most of the paths are good and form part of the Icknield Way. However, one path is not always cleared until the crops are well established, but I have tried to give clear directions. There are no stiles on this walk, part of which involves walking along a very quiet narrow lane for about half-a-mile. Being a shorter walk there are no short cuts but about half the return route involves retracing your steps. The link point to continue on to Hadstock is the station. If you have walked from Stansted this is probably a good place to finish the first day's walking. Strethall is tiny and consists largely of a farm and a church. Parking is possible on the grass near the church, but there are no facilities here.

From Strethall Church **[1]** porch, go to the **left** and exit the churchyard by going down a slope to a path. Turn **left** up this path, passing a pond on your right to join the lane. Keep on the lane beside a line of young horse chestnut trees, to a junction where you turn **left**. The edge of the field on the left is usually planted with corn for pheasants, but on a cold winter's day it is a haven for birds and small animals.

31

Walk 6: Strethall to Great Chesterford

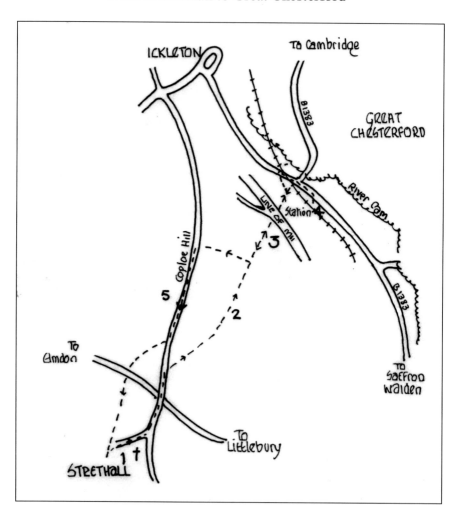

1. Strethall Church - START & FINISH
2. Start of hedged walk
3. Crossing over motorway
4. Great Chesterford station- LINK POINT FOR HADSTOCK
5. Roadside nature reserve

Walk 6: Strethall to Great Chesterford

Stay on this lane over the crossroads, where the other road runs from Littlebury to Elmdon, to the first passing-place on the right along this narrow lane, where there is a bridleway sign pointing across the field on the **right**. Take this path, which is usually marked on the ground, towards a small gap to the left of a larger gap in the hedge - here, turn **left** along the hedged track **[2]** where birds flit in front of you and rabbits try to get trodden on. The noise of the motorway gets louder as you climb towards it. At the motorway fence, turn **right** for a few yards to the footbridge and cross over the busy road **[3]**, then **left** down the other side and **right** along the track. Passing the old smock mill, walk towards the railway, then turn **left** beside the railway up to the road, where you turn **right** over the level crossing into Great Chesterford.

Great Chesterford

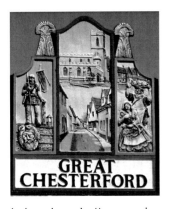

For those on the complete walk over three days, the former Roman town of Great Chesterford (*chester* meaning 'fort') is an ideal place to finish the first day. See the notes in the Introduction regarding accommodation. Both pubs serve food and the village also has a small shop. The bus stops are at the junction after the level crossing. The bus stop on the left currently has an hourly weekday service to Saffron Walden, and on the right to Cambridge (last bus is about 6.30 pm). The daily train service is hourly or better, serving Cambridge, Audley End (2 miles from Saffron Walden), Stansted Mountfitchet and London.

There is nothing visible at the old Roman site, which for a brief period was more important than Colchester. A lot of excavation work was done when the motorway was built, but the best way to have seen parts of the town was in the 17th and 18th centuries, when many of the building materials from the site were used to build the village of Great Chesterford, but none of these houses now exist and the stones are lost. The village still has many interesting buildings which will be seen on the next walk. As with any Roman town, there was a network of roads radiating from it to neighbouring forts and towns. Between Clavering and Duddenhoe End, we came across part of the road to Braughing. Also, after leaving Radwinter the straight road from the Nissen huts to the

Walk 6: Strethall to Great Chesterford

junction is another good example - however, it is less clear beside the old Sampford airfield. The ford in the village name comes from the crossing of the River Granta which, unlike the River Stort crossed several times in earlier walks, runs north through Cambridge and out into The Wash (the Stort heads south into the River Lea and then the Thames near Bow). We will meet the Granta again near its source between Widdington and Henham.

RETURN ROUTE TO STRETHALL

Starting at the station **[4]**, walk down Station Approach to the main road beside small industrial units, including Coles bakery famous for its Christmas puddings. Join the main road and keep **left** beside a new office complex up to the level crossing. You may hear the sound of birdsong from the garden of the old level-crossing keeper's house, and may see an owl or a dove through the thick line of trees. Immediately after crossing the railway, turn **left** beside it along the track signposted Icknield Way. It turns **right** just after a bungalow and becomes a hedged track for a brief period after Smock Mill House. At the fence bordering the motorway, turn **left** up the slope to the footbridge across the busy road, with a non-stop hum of traffic below. Turn **right** for a few yards down to the corner of the field, then **left** along what very soon becomes a hedged track, where the flowers, flitting birds and rabbits soon take your mind off the incessant drone behind you. You stay on this path for about half-a-mile until a track crosses it near the bottom of a gentle slope. Turn **right** at the waymark beside the somewhat gappy hedge up to the lane. Turn **left** down the narrow lane, which is very lightly used by traffic, beside a roadside nature reserve verge **[5]**, and follow the road for just over half-a-mile to the footpath sign on the **right**.

Follow this path across a large field. Once the crops are up, the path is always cleared, but it tends to be difficult to find between ploughing and re-instatement. It is not helped either by the footpath sign pointing at the wrong angle. So if the path is not clear, stand at the road and walk at right angles to the road and this should bring you out at or near a waymark sign beside a hedge at the other side of the field, where you turn **left** up to the lane. Cross the lane and follow this path, with the hedge on your right up to the dead-end road to Strethall, where you turn **right** back to the Church.

Walk Seven: 9 miles   <u>Start TL509425</u>
Great Chesterford to Hadstock

This walk starts at Great Chesterford station, where there is normally space to park, but remember that during the week Station Approach is used by commercial vehicles needing to gain access to the industrial units on the road. It is also possible to park in the village near the school, and if you do, or are starting here on the long walk after a night's rest, it should be easy to pick the route up from the commentary. There are no stiles on this walk. From Great Chesterford Station it will take about 3½ hours to complete the 9 mile walk (4½ miles each way). There are a couple of shorter walk options, the first reducing the walk by more than a half, and the second saving about 30 minutes. There are no shops en route, so it is advisable to stock up at Great Chesterford village shop (down the road on the left after the school). The pub at Hadstock (although closed for a long period) was open again at the time of going to press. Most of the paths are good, with the potentially difficult ones being described in the text - there is road walking at the beginning and you will finish by walking about a mile along the surfaced Cow Lane. Hadstock has very limited public transport to Saffron Walden. The link point to continue to Ashdon is the little village green near the church.

35

Walk 7: Great Chesterford to Hadstock

POINTS A, B & C = SHORTER WALK OPTIONS

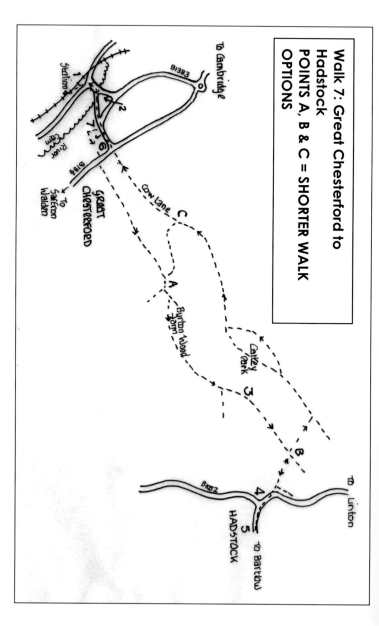

1. Great Chesterford station- START & FINISH
2. Great Chesterford village shop
3. Trig Point – 375 feet
4. The *Kings Head*, Hadstock
5. Hadstock village green – LINK POINT FOR ASHDON
6. The *Plough* pub, Great Chesterford
7. The *Crown & Thistle* pub, Great Chesterford

Walk 7: Great Chesterford to Hadstock

From the station **[1]**, walk down the road beside the industrial units to the main road which sweeps to the right. Cross over the busy road towards the old mill building now converted to flats, and turn **left** along the main road, crossing the River Granta and passing the old mill.

Turn **right** along Church Street towards All Saints Church, but there is only a very narrow footpath along this stretch of the road, so take care. It is well worth diverting into the churchyard, where a look around the base of the tower shows signs that it was moved when the church was shortened in 1891 - the different materials used in the construction of the tower indicate this. The school is on the road to your left and the village shop **[2]** is at the end of the road beyond the school. The houses along this stretch of road are varied and interesting, and there is a small green to the right. Continue on towards the *Crown & Thistle* pub, before turning **right** along Manor Lane past the former almshouses on the corner, then beside some Tudor-style buildings.

At the end of Manor Lane is a modern barn. Go **left** round it, passing a house called 'The Gorse', before taking the track on the **left** up to the busy road. At the road, turn **right** for about 50 yards before crossing it and going up the path opposite. You are once again on the Icknield Way. As you climb, stop and look back from time to time as the view opens up behind you. To the north you can see the new Genome Research Centre and Hinxton Church. To the west the railway and M11 are clearly visible, as are the electricity pylons near Littlebury village. The path becomes more grassy and hedges and trees border the route on your left. The track dips and rises a little before turning sharply to the left and downhill. At this point leave the track and continue **straight ahead** across the field towards the house visible beyond the bushes, continuing to enjoy the views.

Cross the field and go through the gap in the hedge, then over the footbridge to a drive **(Point A)**. Turn **right** and follow the path round to the left into a farmyard at Burtonwood Farm, where you walk between a white house and four barns. The first barn seems to be coming to the end of its life, and the other three reflect developments in barn building over the years. Opposite the fourth barn, turn **right** along a track that can be very muddy, and follow a line of conifers to the corner of the field – here, go through the hedge and bear **left** onto a much better track. The route now takes you beside large arable fields still called Chesterford Common and Hadstock Common, a sign of their past history. Do not enter the copse, but walk along the field-edge as it turns **left**, then **right** at a pond, keeping the ditch to your left and the pylons

Walk 7: Great Chesterford to Hadstock

ahead. The views to the left remain good and no longer include the buildings at the Genome Centre.

You will also notice ahead of you and to your right a selection of buildings which are on land that was briefly used as an airfield during the Second World War. The walk does not go on the airfield site, but the next walk does go close to its border. There are the usual ghost stories of an airman being seen in the night, but nothing to fear during daytime - however, if you happen to see him whilst driving along the road, don't stop to offer a lift, as you'll be shocked to discover he is headless!

At the end of the next field, cross the ditch and go **straight** on. The hedge is now on your right until you go through the next gap, when it reverts to your left again. This hedge marks the county boundary between Essex and Cambridgeshire. Also, along this stretch, you might like to go up to the Trig Point **[3]** which is a little way to the left of the footpath. It is said that on a clear day with good binoculars you can see Ely Cathedral from here!

We are now entering the parish of Hadstock, where a few years ago the parish council had a blitz on their paths and installed some very distinctive waymarks. You can see the parish church over towards the right, nestling in the valley and it won't be long before the larger Cambridgeshire village of Linton comes into view. Soon the path becomes enclosed by hedges and trees on both sides. Flowers bloom in spring, and the sun glints through gaps in the foliage. Once in the open again, you have a choice. If you do *not* wish to visit Hadstock, you can turn **left (Point B)**, since the final part of the route will be retraced on the return journey. If you *do* wish to go to the village, continue for a few yards until you reach a bridge on your **right**, cross the bridge and follow the cross-field path (FP No. 8) to the road.

Just before the road there is a small stable, which used to be a coal merchant's, but now appears to be occupied by a motor mechanic. Also on the left is 'Len's Path', a recently-opened permissive path allowing walkers and cyclists to travel away from vehicles towards Linton.

38

Walk 7: Great Chesterford to Hadstock

Continue in the same direction on the path above the road, which passes the former village shop now selling design drapes and the *Kings Head* pub **[4]**, which recently re-opened after a lengthy closure and is currently serving food once again. The tiny village green **[5]** is just beyond the junction with the road to Saffron Walden. This green is the site of Hadstock's very successful annual village fete, where the village's own brass band performs, and the link point of this section of the walk. Hadstock Church is well worth a visit (for information see next walk).

RETURN ROUTE TO GREAT CHESTERFORD

To return to Great Chesterford, retrace your steps to **Point B**, that is follow the pavement, until the raised footpath on the left takes you to the bend in the road. Leave the road and continue in the same direction, keeping the buildings on your left, across the field and over the footbridge, where you turn **left**, and at the corner of the field turn **right** **(Point B)**. At the top of the field, cut through the gap in the hedge into a large field overlooking a valley. There was a planning application to build a wind farm here (with each of the 10 turbines higher than the London Eye!), but the scheme was rejected on appeal.

Walk 7: Great Chesterford to Hadstock

Continue in the same direction down the field until you are under the electricity cables – here, turn **left** and walk towards the bottom left corner of the field where a waymark post may be visible - the path is usually clearly marked. Cross the bridge and follow the path across the next field in roughly the same direction, to a track at the top corner of the field. Turn **left** along the track up the hill. After about 300 yards, you may see a pillbox on your right (if not buried in undergrowth) - a few yards further on, go through the gap in the hedge into the next field. The path crosses diagonally to a bridge on the far side, where a yellow mark on a post may be seen. Before you get to the bridge, look back to your left and you may see the ruins of a house called Catley Park.

Cross the bridge and follow the path inside the wood, and then to the right of the hedge to another small wood. At the end of this wood, go through a gap in the hedge on your **left** and down the hill, with the woodland still on your left. At the bottom, turn **right** onto the Icknield Way bridleway and follow, firstly the grass path and then, at Crave Hall after a gate, the surfaced track above Grumble Hall in the valley along Cow Lane. **Point C** is before the Little Paddocks (which is a house and kennels). After a mile along this lane, you will reach the main road. Take care in crossing the road before following the High Street beside the *Plough* pub **[6]**, and on towards the *Crown & Thistle* **[7]**, before retracing your steps to the station. Do not rush down this road as it is worth spending time looking at the houses and the clever way the newer buildings have been blended in with the old.

SHORTER OPTIONS

1. At **Point A** turn left down the drive before reaching Burtonwood Farm and this leads you out onto Cow Lane **(Point C)**, where you turn left back to Great Chesterford. If you are doing the shorter walk from Hadstock, turn left at the track before Little Paddocks **(Point C)** and climb the hill to pick up the route at **Point A**, where the footbridge is on your right.

2. At **Point B** turn left after leaving the hedged path and pick up the instructions from **Point B** on the return route.

Walk Eight: 8 miles
Hadstock to Ashdon

Start TL560448

Hadstock is a tiny village with a population of about 300. It has an interesting church well worth a visit. The return section of this walk can include a visit to a restored windmill, and there is an ancient burial site just off the route. The walk starts at the little village green [1] where there is limited car parking. However, if there are no events on at the village hall, you could go up the drive to the left of the church and park behind the hall. The walk will take about 3 hours to complete the 8 miles (3 miles to Ashdon and 5 miles back). This is a true circular walk and there are no short cuts other than retracing your steps. There is a little shop in Ashdon open 5 days a week, as well as a pub. Ashdon Museum is open on Wednesdays and Sundays during the summer and serves refreshments, and there is also a pub a little off-route in Bartlow, The *Kings Head* [2] in Hadstock (the other side of the junction) is currently open and serving food. The outward walk is mainly on paths, but the route back includes tracks and a fairly long road stretch from Bartlow. Ashdon has a limited bus service (route 59) linking Saffron Walden to Haverhill, but nothing going to Hadstock. The link point to continue on to Radwinter is the pub in Ashdon.

From the green [1], walk beside Waylands up the drive to the ancient church, passing the thatched house called Beam Ends, which appears to have a modern extension hiding what could be some interesting plasterwork. Take the left-hand track towards the village hall and, at the end of the stone wall, turn **left** through a gap into the meadow. There is a notice board here reporting on the results of some archaeological and geophysical surveys conducted in 2005.

The original Church of St Botolph was allegedly built by King Canute in 1020 as a Minster to celebrate his victory over Edmund Ironside at Assandun. However, some historians dispute that Assandun was in the present neighbouring parish of Ashdon, but think it was elsewhere in Essex. The doubts over its origins do not alter the fact that the church has a Saxon door. Another possible basis of this church's foundation is that Hadstock could be the lost settlement of *Icanho*, where in AD654 the Abbot Botolph founded a monastery. In 870 it was damaged by raiding Danes, and may have remained in poor condition until Canute chose to rebuild it 150 years later.

41

Walk 8: Hadstock to Ashdon

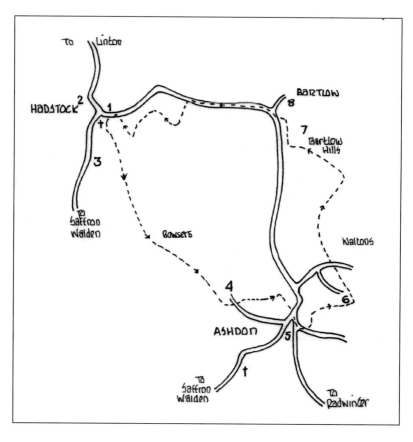

1. Hadstock village green – START & FINISH
2. The *Kings Head* pub
3. Site of wartime airfield
4. Ricketts Farm
5. *Rose & Crown* and shop – LINK POINT FOR RADWINTER
6. Ashdon windmill
7. Bartlow Hills – Tumulus
8. *Three Hills* pub, Bartlow

Cross the meadow and climb over the stile, where the waymark shows the path crossing the field towards a telegraph pole in the far corner of the field. There have been times when this cross-field path has not been cleared, and it appears that the landowner prefers you to turn **left** and walk round the edge of the field to the second ditch, crossing on the left near a telegraph pole. Cross the ditch and walk diagonally to your right up the hill in the direction of the waymark - you will pass about 15 yards to the right of a lone tree, before reaching the top of the field. Look back occasionally to your left to enjoy the view, and you may get your first sighting of the recently-restored Ashdon Windmill. At the top of the hill, cross into the next field and stay in the same direction along path 21 across the field to the right-hand corner of a wood ahead.

To your right is the site of the former wartime airfield **[3]** of Little Walden. It was built in 1943 as Station 165 for the 9th US Army Air Force. Initially, it was the base for the 409th Bomb Group until September 1944, then housed the 8th Air Force 361 Fighter Group with their yellow-nosed Mustangs - this group gave support to their units based in France. In March 1945, the airfield once again housed bombers when the 493rd Group moved in whilst their main airfield was being repaired. It was relinquished in November 1945 and finally closed in 1958. Many of the buildings are still standing and there is a story of a reclusive eccentric army major living in those buildings for several years until he suddenly vanished. The road linking Saffron Walden with Hadstock was closed whilst the airfield was operational and Ordnance Survey maps dated in the 1950s still show the road as closed.

The wood you are approaching also continues to provide evidence of its proximity to the airfield, housing a pill box and, until recently, some old ironmongery. It is a private wood so walk to the **right** of it towards what appears to be another fearsome object. The object is not a guillotine from the French Revolution, but a very high gate designed to keep the chickens in what is becoming a small orchard. Go through the gate and down the hill, as you watch the poultry enjoying their freedom outdoors. Keep their home well to your left, to another high gate and a track. If the chickens decide to chase you, thinking you are a bringer of food, you may find your skills tested to keep them in the field when you leave. You are now at Bowsers, where the main house was built in the 17th century. Climb over the stile opposite and walk across a narrow strip of land, keeping the grassy mound to your right. This brings you to another stile which comes out onto another track. Cross this track to enter a wood near a huge, newly-built tree house. Once out on the other side, you will see a stile at the **left**-hand corner of the meadow.

Continue in the same direction onto the tarmac drive, passing The Red House, where you may spot some cars from the 1950s.

At the junction turn **left** between a house and a barn, after which the map shows a field-edge path. It appears that the preferred route is to stay on the track to the other end of the field and join the waymarked track on the **right** which goes in our desired direction of travel. The track crosses a bridge and follows a tributary of the River Bourn, passing the Ashdon pumping station, with a wood on the other side of the stream. Go through the stile, and continue to follow the stream down to a waymarked bridge on your **left**. Cross the bridge and the field (where there may be cattle), down to the opposite bottom corner, where you climb up and turn **right** along a quiet lane (if you were to follow this lane the other way, it would lead to the 17th century house at Ricketts Farm **[4]**).

After a few yards take the path on the **left** through the woods, which after a while follows a hedge towards Newnham Hall Farm – historically, one of the manors of Ashdon. Just before reaching the farm, turn **right** over the stile and up the side of the field with the hedge on your left. Go into the next field, where the path turns slightly to the **left** and beside some paddocks, towards a bridge over a ditch into a meadow offering fine views towards the windmill and the countryside to the north.

Turning **right** here takes you down to a small gate which leads to Dorvis Lane. Follow the lane down to the main road, where you turn **right** beside the multi-coloured cottages of Collier Row and the school. On the opposite side of the road are some seats, allotments and a war memorial. The *Rose & Crown* pub **[5]** and the shop are a little further down the road at the junction.

ASHDON

Ashdon is a scattered settlement with a population of less than a thousand. It is served by the River Bourn which joins up near Bartlow with one of the many rivers called Granta, all of which come together before Cambridge. Much of the trading activity of the village has traditionally been conducted around the junction of the Radwinter road, where the pub, shop, nursery and garage remain. Nearby is the village museum. We will walk up Radwinter Road on both the return route to Hadstock and the next leg to Radwinter, and the names of the cottages tell us that just how thriving this area was. White Horse House on the corner and the Old Fox were two of the village's four pubs that have now closed, and The Old Bakery and The Maltings add to the history, whilst Willow Cottage has a note under the sign stating that was formally a butcher's shop. Interestingly, the church is at the top of the hill beyond the nursery, as is the Guildhall. Ashdon has four or five weekday buses linking Saffron Walden to Haverhill.

RETURN ROUTE TO HADSTOCK

Whether you are returning to Hadstock or continuing on to Radwinter, walk up Radwinter Road opposite the pub beside the recently extended village hall with various best-kept village plaques outside. Several of the houses mentioned above are along this stretch of road, and you will also pass the Baptist Church. It is opposite the large church car park that you turn **left** into Kates Lane, and to return to Hadstock you turn **left** again along path 107 over a stream soon after passing Chapel Farm. Climb round the field, keeping it on your right as it turns at the top of the hill, where there is a place to sit and admire the village from above. Keep the hedge on your left as you cut through the bushes at the end of the first field, ignoring the paths to your right, you will soon see the recently restored windmill **[6]**. At the end of the third field, cut down to a hedged bridleway and turn

45

Walk 8: Hadstock to Ashdon

left up the track *(it appears that people keep to the field to the left of the track if it is too muddy)* towards the windmill and a couple of cottages. There has been a windmill on this site since 1757, and there is a photo dated as recently as 1932, showing the mill with sails, which it has once again.

Ignore the first footpath signs opposite the windmill and walk a few yards further down the track to the lower entrance of the windmill, where you turn **right** through the mill car park. Take the cross-field path which goes at an angle of about 30 degrees towards the left of the houses ahead. This path is usually cleared and at the bottom there is a new stile to cross into a meadow where you keep to the right until you reach a gate and a stile to take you to the road.

Enter Waltons opposite along the main path, where you are asked to keep dogs on a lead to avoid disturbing the horses. If it is spring, don't miss noticing the beauty of spring flowers that adorn the area opposite the impressive house of Waltons - it is worth a wander up the drive just to see the flowers.

At the top of the drive, stay in the same direction crossing various tracks onto a grassy path, which goes along the top of two large fields with views over the Bourn valley towards Linton. At the end of the second field near the top of the hill, turn **left** down the track beside a hedge towards a long narrow grove of trees. We are now on the Bartlow Estate.

Just before you reach the road, take the track on the **right** towards Three Hills Farm and pass a circular former water tower and some cottages. Bear **left** at the dovecote beside the children's nursery and then, just before the road, take the footpath through the trees on the **right**. The path ends just before the old railway line where, if you wish to visit Barlow Hills **[7]**, turn **right** to the ancient burial mounds. There were once seven, but over many years they have been reduced and pillaged, and one was apparently demolished to make way for the railway line from Haverhill to Cambridge. After visiting the site, retrace your steps to the road.

The direct route entails a **left** turn at the path junction, and **right** at the road. The house sign opposite reads 'Booking Hall', and when you cross the old railway line you can see why. Unfortunately we now have some road walking, and also will be leaving Essex for some of the road walking section. Bartlow used to be a railway junction where trains from Audley End and Saffron Walden terminated, and the Stour Valley Line operated through trains

46

Walk 8: Hadstock to Ashdon

between Cambridge and Colchester. Part of the latter line still exists near Castle Hedingham, where you can travel on a mile or so of track behind a steam engine. The road passes the brick supports of the old railway bridge, and on towards the 30 mph speed limit sign, after which turn **left** on the lane signposted Hadstock 1½ miles. (For the *Three Hills* pub **[8]** in Bartlow, stay straight on for a few hundred yards).

The route passes the recreation ground with a solitary goal, where the annual fete is held. On the right is a building that looks like an old school but was probably stables, and now appear to be kennels. Stay on the road beside another relic of the old railway. The road now goes under another old railway bridge and out into the countryside where a large sign welcomes you back into Essex. Be careful because, even though there are very few cars, they can be going fast. The fields on the right are generally flat and hide the course of the River Granta before it joins up with two other rivers of the same name on the outskirts of Cambridge.

The lane is pleasant and is bordered in spring by wild flowers and in autumn wild fruits. After about ¾ mile you will go over a bridge and see a brick water holder with a corrugated iron roof - pass that and a couple of cottages and take the wide track on your **left**. Pass the small wood on your left before taking the path on your **right** (path 31). This follows the line of a hedge and the edge of another wood before reaching an open field. Stay in the same direction over the field, until you reach the right-hand corner of a hedge, then keep to the right of the hedge to the next gap on your **left,** where you cross the bridge. (If you want to head straight back to the village, turn right for a few yards to the road then turn left along it back to the start). Otherwise, turn **left** after the bridge along the track, known as Siggin's Lane, beside a tennis court to the top, where you bear **right** and continue beside a large field. At the bridleway (which can be a little muddy), turn **right** to the end where you turn **left** on the lane back to the village green at Hadstock.

Walk Nine: 9¼ miles
Ashdon to Radwinter

Start TL586421

Ashdon is a small village with a population of less than a thousand, about three miles from Saffron Walden. It is served about five times a day by buses linking Saffron Walden and Haverhill. It has a small village shop open five days a week, a thriving pub and a nursery. On a Wednesday or Sunday afternoon (apart from winter) you can visit the museum, and learn more of the history of the village. This walk, which starts at the pub in Ashdon, is one of the longer walks in the book: allow at least 3¾ hours for the full distance (5 miles out and 4¼ miles back). There is one short cut which reduces the walk to about 5 miles. At the time of writing, *The Plough* in Radwinter is closed and its future is uncertain. The walk starts along a very quiet lane and follows paths and tracks including cross-field paths to Radwinter. There can be problems in the Bendysh Woods if forestry work is being conducted, and the path out of Radwinter End does tend to get overgrown through lack of use. On the return route the paths are good, but it may be difficult to cross the young River Bourn at the ford after heavy rain - an alternative route has been described. Radwinter has a very limited bus service which does not serve Ashdon. The link point to continue to Thaxted is Radwinter School.

Start at Crown Hill outside the Rose & Crown **[1]**, which is the only survivor of five pubs once found in and around the village. Cross the road and walk up the hill towards Radwinter, passing the village hall and the site of the White Horse which closed as long ago as 1905. Of the other pubs, the Fox and Lamb closed in the 1950s and the Bricklayers long ago. Many of the houses in Radwinter Road also tell of their past, and as recently as the 1980s there were two general stores and a butcher's shop. The Baptist Church is on your left, but the Parish Church and Guildhall are at the top of Crown Hill, as they were built long before the village moved down the hill to the River Bourn.

Walk 9: Ashdon to Radwinter

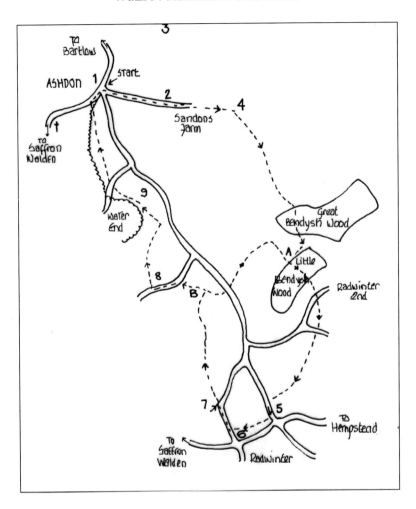

1. *Rose & Crown* and shop –
START & FINISH
2. Kates Lane
3. Ashdon Windmill
4. Winsey Farm
5. Former Baptist Church

6. Radwinter School – LINK
POINT FOR THAXTED
7. Ford
8. Ashdon Farm
9. Ford

POINTS A & B – SHORTER WALK OPTIONS

Walk 9: Ashdon to Radwinter

Opposite the Baptist Church car park, turn **left** along Kates Lane **[2]**, but before doing so take a look at the next house on the right, the 16th century residence called New Sandons. Kates Lane is very quiet with a wooded stream on the left and an occasional cottage, including Kates Cottage, probably named after the road. To the right are arable fields and as you walk along, on the left you may catch glimpses of the sails of the recently restored Ashdon Windmill **[3]**, visited on walk 8.

After nearly a mile, go through the gate and pass a couple of ponds before walking to the left of Old Sandons (named after John de Sandon recorded in 1303). The building is not as striking as New Sandons, but has the feel of a peaceful home. Most of the land and buildings we pass on this walk were once owned by the Countess of Warwick (King Edward VII's mistress), and sold off by auction towards the end of the 19th century.

After passing the buildings, the surfaced track swings to the right, but you should stay in the same direction on the grassy track, where on the right you will pass three fields (the second being very large), whilst on the left are more trees. Ignore the next track on your left and continue to the corner where you go through a gap in the hedge on your **right**, then up the hill beside the telegraph poles, keeping the hedge to your right. As you climb, the trees of Great Bendysh Wood come into view.

At the top of the hill is the site of Winsey Farm **[4]**. The derelict farm has now been demolished and a large new house built. However, in 1553 it was the home of Humphrey de Wyneleshey, from whom came its name. In 1851 the farm employed four men and a boy farming 130 acres, but this was not enough to fully support farmer Fuller Tredgett and his family of eight children under 11 who still had to apply for poor relief.

A new wooden fence has been erected around the property and the route follows the fence to the right. There is a cross-field path to your **right** starting on the final left turn of the fence - this path is not always reinstated as promptly as it should be, so follow it towards a wooden waymark post to your right at the bottom of the field by a plank bridge. The waymark on the bridge points in the direction of the path to another plank bridge (which does not have a waymark post) - cross it and continue in the same direction to a third bridge. You then turn **left** to pass an old tree and a pond with water lilies in flower during summer. You then bear **right** onto a track towards a distant farmhouse. After about 200 yards, turn **left** onto a waymarked path, and cross the field.

At the far end enter Great Bendysh Wood by way of a footbridge. Such woodlands are rare in Essex - only 3.15 per cent of the land in this county is designated woodland, compared with a national average of 5.4 per cent. Stay on the ride, a wide grass track where there has been recent tree clearance work and in spring you can admire the orchids. In these woods there used to be a fire-watch point that very much resembled an umpire's chair from Wimbledon, but it now appears to have been removed and replaced by more orthodox towers. Bendysh was a settlement over a thousand years ago, but now all that survives of the name are two woods and Bendysh Hall. The woods were used for hunting, and you can still see deer in the area, but both this and Little Bendysh Wood are now managed by the Forestry Commission, and from time to time proof of their activity can be seen with the paths being churned up.

Stay on the path until it turns to the left and then after about 50 yards turn **right** to leave the wood. Keep to the left of the hedge, until you reach Little Bendysh Wood, where you turn **right** along the field edge beside the wood. Stay beside the wood for some time and cross a footbridge on your **left (Point A)** into the woods where, if there are no aircraft around, you may like to stop and listen, enjoying the silence. Follow the track and leave the wood over a bridge to a field. Walk across the field, where there are views towards Saffron Walden to the right, to a cottage with a beech hedge and the tiny hamlet of Radwinter End.

Turn **right** along the lane, passing a house called Little Gates with two small gates, then past a residence called The Cliff - definitely not a feature of this part of Essex! But a fox above the name indicates something that might be seen. After Willow House, turn **left** along path 34. The route of this path has recently been in dispute, but is now fairly clear, although still liable to become overgrown. (If it does prove difficult to negotiate, stay on the very quiet lane and turn **left** at the junction until you reach a clump of trees on the right, then follow the footpath through the trees.) If path 34 is good, follow it as directed to a ditch and onto the cross-field path; if the cross-field path is not clear, aim to the left of the bush at the top of the field beyond the next bridge. If there has been rain the soil will cling to your boots, but it is only a short distance to the bridge, which you cross and turn **right** following the ditch to the lane. Cross the lane and go through a tiny spinney onto a field-edge path, initially arable, then meadowland, staying to the left of the fields. Part of this stretch may be overgrown, and it is also the only section of this walk with stiles. The river on your left is a tributary of the River Pant which becomes the Blackwater in the Braintree area. The final large meadow before reaching the road has several jumps for horses - keep to the path which is clearly defined.

At the road turn **left** beside an old orchard and Mill End Cottage. (*The Plough*, if re-opened, is the only pub in Radwinter and is opposite the end of this lane, so after visiting it you will need to retrace your steps.) Just before the former Baptist Church **[5]**, built in 1850 and finally closed in 1998, look for a second SLOW sign on the road. Take the footpath on your right beside a new fence, where there used to be glasshouses, then besides some farm buildings until you reach a fence. Turn **right** into a field, then **left** down to the river.

Cross the bridge and climb up the other side to the left of the end house, then follow the narrow path beside the school playing field. Turn **right** into a cul-de-sac, then **left** up to a lane and a seat near the junction. For Radwinter School **[6]**, car park and link point to continue to Thaxted turn **left** along the lane for a few yards.

RETURN ROUTE TO ASHDON

To continue to Thaxted or visit the village centre and church turn left at the road by the seat, but to return to Ashdon turn **right** along this lane towards the speed de-restriction signs and a ford **[7]**, where the lane turns sharply to the right. Leave the road and continue straight

on along path 52, keeping the hedge to
your right, except when you cross a
narrow field to some fine oaks, after
which the hedge is to your right again
and you cross a bridleway. Eventually
the path veers to the left beside a narrow
stretch of woodland. Just after the next
hedge on the left, there is a small gap on
the **right** between two taller trees where
you enter a wood. Turn **left** onto a wider
path and when it turns left (just before an
almost hidden old storage tank in the
woods), turn **right** on a faint path and
through a gap in the wire fence onto the
cross-field path. This is usually clearly
marked (if not follow the tram lines),
towards the left of a solitary bush-like
tree **(Point B)**. Here you turn **left** to cross

the same field (this is usually marked, but not always!), towards the
corner of a wood called Tilekiln Grove, which you keep on your left
until you reach the lane, where you turn **left** again.

Follow the lane round for about ½ mile to Ashdon Farm **[8]**,
where you turn **right** along the drive, then **left** in front of Red Rose
Barn, a converted barn with a sheep weather-vane. Then go to the
left of the pond onto a hedged track for about ½ mile – from here,
once again you may get glimpses of the windmill. When the hedge
on the left ends and a view over an open field opens up, turn **left**
along another hedged track for about 125 yards, possibly beside
some pheasant feeding stations - there is a small gap in the hedge
here on the **right** to cut through. There should be a waymark here,
but if not, it is easy to pass (it is just beyond a large oak tree on the
left and near a tree that appears to be shorn of its bark). Turn **right**
and cross the wide field edge, which is occasionally used to grow
pheasant food, and follow the path down to the right of the
coniferous wood below. At the time of writing there was a sign at the
bottom of the path which read, 'No Horses, Footpath and Beetle
Bank'.

Pass the wood and turn **left** along the grass path towards
the River Bourn and a ford **[9]**. Cross the ford and turn **right** beside
the river to Water End. (Sometimes after heavy rain the ford may be
difficult to cross - if so, retrace your steps, then continue to the road,

turn **left** up the lane past Mallards then turn **left** along the little lane until a sharp **left** turn where the bridleway on the right goes towards White Cottage.) Water End is one of seven 'Ends' in Ashdon and is noted for its gardens. This is the most remote of the 'Ends', and started life as a clearing in the woods near the source of the River Bourn. Turn **right** at the road until it starts to climb and turn right – here, bear **left** along the bridleway beside White Cottage, then turn **right** up the slope, keeping the river to your left.

Stay on this path for the final mile or so back to the village, crossing a garden with a pond before going to the left of a barn. The path then can be a little muddy as you approach the next cottage, but the woods going down to the river are so attractive that you can almost forget about the slippery surface. After passing the cottage, continue beside the river to a spot where it used to be bridged three times, but after the heavy rains in 2007, these bridges were washed away, so look for a point where the path splits and take the **right** one just above the bushes. Follow the new path by the fence, turning **left** to cross a bridge where the path on your right brings you out beside Ashdon Museum. Turn right at the road for the pub.

SHORTER WALK OPTION

At **Point A** do not enter the wood but continue beside it for a hundred yards or so to the end of the field, where there may be pheasant feeding stations - there is also a wide track leaving the wood at this point. Turn **right** here across the field to a ditch where there is a crossing point, then turn **left** keeping the ditch on your left until you reach the garden of a house. The path goes to the left of the house, but it appears that most people sensibly stay in the field and go round to the **right** of the house to the road. Cross over the road and follow the signposted path up to a solitary tree like bush where you turn **right** at **Point B** towards Tilekiln Grove.

If doing the shorter walk from Radwinter, after crossing the field **(Point B)**, turn **right** to the tree, and follow the path down to the lane which you cross and enter the field opposite. Keep the house to your right, and follow the ditch to within a couple of hundred yards of Great Bendysh Wood, where you cross the ditch on your **right** before walking between the two fields to Little Bendysh Wood, where you turn **left** beside the wood and **right** over the bridge **(Point A)**.

54

Walk Ten: 12 miles
Radwinter to Thaxted

Radwinter is a compact village with the school, church and village hall all clustered around the same junction. This area has historically been the centre of trade, with the road going down beside the church not only housing the last village shop, but also home to many other traders. Now, whilst it still has a Post Office, the future of its sparse bus service and the former village pub are often discussed. This circular walk is the longest in the book and starts at Radwinter School [1]. There is a car park opposite at the playing fields. You need to allow at least 4½ hours for the full walk of 12 miles (5 miles out and 7 miles back), so I have outlined two link routes to make it suitable for all abilities. It is recommended that you allow a whole day for a leisurely walk, so that lunch can be taken in Thaxted where there are pubs, cafes and shops and a Friday market. The walk is mainly on good paths and some very quiet lanes. The return route does not go through West Wood, because the paths can be very muddy, but if you do wish to go that way, the route is described in the box on page 60. If you are doing the whole of the Uttlesford Way, it is recommended that you finish the second day at Thaxted, where there is accommodation and bus route No 5 serves Saffron Walden weekdays until early evening. The link point if you are continuing onto Debden is the Guildhall.

Leave the car park [2] at the playing fields, where the cricket pavilion is on the site of a windmill, and join the road opposite the school where you turn **right** here at the link point from the Ashdon walk and pass the village hall. Cross the road to the church [3], which is very interesting with several unique treasures assembled during the 19th century when it had five successive vicars from the same family. Because of the value of these treasures, the church is usually locked but there is a regular open morning, currently the first Saturday of the month. The church was also, controversially, ornately decorated during its repairs in 1638, but the Puritans systematically destroyed this work over the next few years in line with Cromwell's instructions.

Walk back to the junction where, on the other side of the road, the Great Fire of Radwinter started in 1874. It spread very quickly, damaging much of the centre of the village and threatening the church. Many cottages and trade premises were destroyed, but the church was untouched and nobody lost their life.

Walk 10: Radwinter to Thaxted

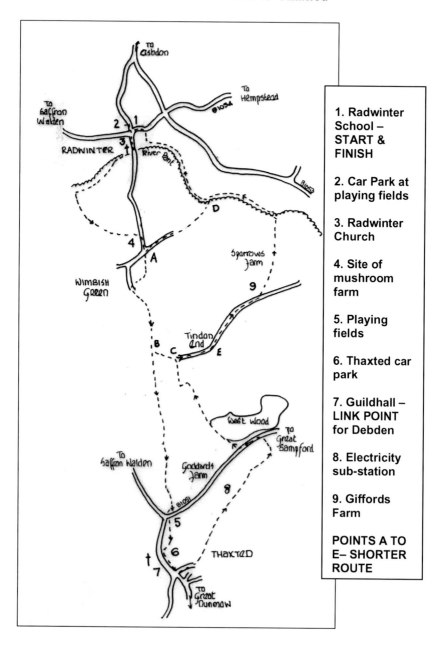

1. Radwinter School – START & FINISH

2. Car Park at playing fields

3. Radwinter Church

4. Site of mushroom farm

5. Playing fields

6. Thaxted car park

7. Guildhall – LINK POINT for Debden

8. Electricity sub-station

9. Giffords Farm

POINTS A TO E– SHORTER ROUTE

56

Walk 10: Radwinter to Thaxted

When you consider the methods used to fight fires at that time, this was a great achievement. The village soon recovered from the fire, and by 1900 Radwinter supported two blacksmiths, a saddler and a wheelwright/carpenter, as well as a post office/ tobacconist, a tailor, two butchers, two bakers plus a general store and brewer – all this to support a population of 600.

Walk down Church Hill for a few yards and turn **right** along the footpath 68 below the churchyard. This takes you through a gate into Church Meadow where you will pass some bramble bushes - after passing the Millennium Seat the path runs between a fence and the river. Go past a concrete bridge and continue in the same direction until you reach a hump bridge on the **left** near a hedge.

Cross this bridge and walk the short distance across the meadow before turning **right**, keeping the hedge to your left until the far corner of this large meadow. In 1874 these meadows would have been occupied by livestock, as at that time there were over 1,100 sheep, nearly 800 lambs and more than 800 pigs in the parish. Now you will have to wait until you are nearly back in Radwinter before any possibility of seeing any cows or sheep. In 1874 mangolds were planted on 98 acres to feed all that livestock.

At the far corner, slip through the hedge over a bridge and up the hill with the woodland and hedges on your left. After two more bridges there is more woodland, the ground is covered in both these wooded areas with bluebells and dogs mercury. The spire of Radwinter Church can be seen through the hedge as you walk beside a very large field.

You will now see some dilapidated Nissen huts **[4]** ahead of you and, after crossing the fence and going round some hedges, you will be amongst them. After the war a mushroom farm was started here by ex-Polish airmen and it is thought that the huts were moved here from the prisoner-of-war camp at Radwinter Manor. Don't leave the path as the huts are in a poor state and contain asbestos. Duck under the gate to the road. This is a Roman road and forms part of the ancient route from Great Chesterford to Chelmsford - it will form the backbone of our walk to Thaxted.

Turn **right**, passing Radwinter House which was built at the same time as the mushroom farm was developed and was originally called Warsaw House. On the opposite side of the road was an air raid shelter which was part of the Great Sampford Airfield Defence System. At the junction **(Point A)**, turn **right** until you reach the second telegraph pole, where you turn **left** onto footpath 37. This is where ancient and modern history merge, as you are walking on a Roman road beside a WW2 airfield.

Modern meddling also comes into play here, because the footpath does not follow the ancient way on the border of the airfield all the way - that would be too simple! We have to divert into a corner of Wimbish Green. After about 250 yards, between the second and third electricity poles, look out for a footbridge hidden in the bushes on the **right**. Cross the bridge, then a field, to come out onto a lane immediately to the right of a cottage.

Turn **left** along the lane and straight on to a track, where you will pass a cottage with the unusual name of 'Joe on the Donkey' - this used to be a post office, so maybe there was a donkey carrying postman Joe's mail! This building was also once an off-licence, so it has had an interesting past. There are a couple more houses before the top of the lane. The house at the top, where you turn **left**. used to be the roadman's house and the track up to it was lined with relics of the days when every village was responsible for its own highways. The final cottage has a warning about dogs.

After that cottage you go through the gate ahead of you, and take the hedged path on the **right** which, after coming out of the bushes, takes you down to a footbridge. Cross the bridge and the next field, towards some trees and a drive. As you gently descend, you will see the spire of Thaxted Church for the first time.

Follow the drive to a crossing of tracks **(Point B)**. For Thaxted, go straight across the track and up the hill. The water tower at Cutlers Green comes into view on your right. Stay on the left of the overgrown Christmas tree plantation which is reached after crossing a bridge - Bow Croft Wood is now to your left. Leave the plantation staying on a good track, however you do not stay on it for long. Just before the track on the left, turn **left** at a waymark onto a field-edge path. This path, which can be quite narrow, is to the left of the hedge. Walk through two fields before you cross to the right of the hedge and join a track. Some years this farmer grows blue borage and linseed on these fields. Cross the ditch into the next field, taking the waymarked path diagonally across the fields, aiming to the right of the church. As you cross the fields, the ironwork of the bridge comes into view under some trees. Cross the bridge and continue to the bushes by the ditch – here, take the second path diagonally left across the field to a telegraph pole.

Cross the track and climb up the hill to a new bridge over a ditch, with steps up the other side into the next field, to come out on the road at its top right-hand corner. You are now on the outskirts of Thaxted. Turn **right** past a drive, where there used to be a sign reading 'POOZ R US' (free horse manure), and after a new housing development on the left, go through the woodland to the playing fields **[5]**. Keep to the right of the pavilion, before turning **left** and **right** on the roads to a footpath* beside housing and the day centre, onto Margaret Street just above the car park **[6]**. To reach the town centre and Guildhall **[7]**, walk along Bell Lane to the end. The link point in Thaxted if continuing on to Debden is the Guildhall, just down from the Church.

*The footpath may be overgrown, in which case it may be better to stay on the roads.

RETURN ROUTE TO RADWINTER

The return route is the longest leg in the book, partly because a more direct route through West Wood and along a bridleway (which is about ¾ mile shorter) can be extremely muddy, even after a dry spell. If you wish to risk this route it is described on the next page.

From the Guildhall cross the road and walk down the hill past the Post Office. Turn **left** into Town Street, then The Tanyard, which soon changes its name to Copthall Lane. After passing Walnut Meadow House, bear **left** into the meadow and follow a well-walked path over towards the trees on the left of the meadow. Where the path dips towards the ditch, cross the first bridge but not the second, then climb back up away from the ditch and onto the path on the left of the field.

Cross over the next ditch to leave the field, and then turn **left** for a short distance to the top of this field, where you turn **right** to the electricity sub-station **[8]**. Stay to the right of the sub-station fence, and at its end continue up to the pylon and bear **right** along the cross-field

59

path to the corner of the hedge ahead, where you cross the bridge and stay beside the ditch until you meet a grass track. This swings to the left and then goes between two houses to the road with Spriggs Farm opposite.

Turn **left** on the main road and pass the children's pre-school to Tilehall Farm. Immediately after the next farm building, turn **right** along the footpath beside a couple of ponds and the farmhouse up to some barns. It can be a little muddy here as you walk to the right of the barns, but the track is wide all the way up to the wood and it is easy to avoid the puddles. This is the western edge of West Wood and, except for the wooden fencing, is a very natural wood to walk beside. Stay to the right of the next three fields, then a couple of houses come into view. At the far corner of the third field, turn **left** along a farm track up to a large outbuilding. Turn **right** here beside a third house and through a gap in the fence to a track. (For a shorter walk back to Thaxted turn left after going through the gap **[Point C]**.) Otherwise for Radwinter continue straight on along a very good drive, through a gate and up to Market Farm at Tindon End.

You may notice some Turpin's Trail markers along this stretch - this is a figure-of-eight walk linking Dick Turpin's birthplace (Hempstead) to the town where he worked as a butcher (Thaxted), via Great Sampford. After Market Farm our route becomes a road and passes a very pleasant wooded part of the estate of Tindon Manor, which has a large variety of trees, plants and habitats (including a pond with an island) visible from the road. Opposite is Gamekeepers House which is also worth admiring.

West Wood Route: This shorter route can be very muddy and difficult on the pitted bridleway, where the drainage is poor - this route can also be difficult even after a dry spell. If you wish to follow it, turn **right** along the road at Spriggs Farm until you reach the entrance to West Wood on your **left** (the name being derived from Wet Wood). Enter the nature reserve, and stay on the main track as it **turns right** in the wood, beside a pond and out to meet a track. Turn **right** and **left** along this hedged path, until you meet the lane near Tindon End, where you turn **right** along the road **(Point E)**. Being a nature reserve, it is an attractive woodland with its spring flowers and wildlife, ranging from deer to great crested newts. It is an SSSI and managed by the Essex Wildlife Trust.

On the right you pass the bridleway from West Wood **(Point E)**. There are several little lanes like this in this area which just lead to a couple of houses, they make easy peaceful walking but are not traffic free. A little further along you pass Dove House Farm (built 1534), which has an attractive duck pond. The road winds a little here and then climbs to a small wood on the right - soon after that take the track on the **left** to Giffords Farm **[9]**, an attractive timber and plaster house with 19th century casement windows and a chimney with the date 1626 on it.

The drive becomes a grass bridleway soon after passing the house, and offers a fine view of Great Sampford down in the valley. At the end of this track, we turn **left** and finally leave Turpin's Trail. This signposted footpath 17 is another road that leads to just a single house and half-way down, just in case you found the descent tiring, there is an old seat where you can sit and enjoy the view towards Hempstead and its church tower, if the hedges are not too high.

The road ends at Sparrows Hall, but you continue downwards on a hedged path to the end of the garden. Here you bend slightly to the **right** to follow the field edge down to the river, where you cross the bridge and cut **left** across the meadow into the next field to generally follow the River Pant upstream. Like many rivers this far upstream, it was used for trade up until the Middle Ages. The Pant becomes the Blackwater at Braintree and reaches the sea near Mersea Island after passing Maldon. It is difficult to see how boats could get up here without grounding, but in those days the vessels would not be large.

After going over a stile, the path climbs away from the river and on your right is the new Gorse Wood, set in just under three acres consisting mostly of oak, but with a total of nearly 3,000 native trees and bushes. It was planted in 1995 and some of the quicker growing varieties are already beginning to mature.

Before the top of the field to your left is a hidden waymark, where you slip down beside a hawthorn bush to enter the next meadow. Stay along the top of the field, before leaving it at the bottom far corner, after passing a pumping station. The path now follows the river among mature woodland trees. The full route ignores the bridge **(Point D)** and continues to the right of the river for some distance. Cattle and sheep may be grazing in any of these fields. Pass two more river bridges on your left. Eventually you cross a concrete bridge over a tributary keep to the left of the new wooden building and leave the field through a small

Walk 10: Radwinter to Thaxted

gate. Turn **right** up the path to the road where you **turn left** into the village and at the village hall **right** back to the car park.

SHORTER WALK OPTIONS

1. From **Point A** turn **left** along the quiet lane towards the Brockholds Farm, follow the lane down and up to a point where it turns right and peters out. At this point go **left** for a few yards, then **right** on the footpath beside the pill box, towards the left of the hedge and Clay Wood. As you descend you will see the valley of the River Pant, and then cross the bridge before turning **left (Point D).**

If returning to Thaxted without visiting Radwiinter, at the far end of the woodland is a bridge **(Point D)**. Cross the bridge and climb the field edge, turning **left** and **right** as you approach the pill box and see Mortlocks Farm on your right. After the pillbox, turn **left** for a few yards then **right** along another very quiet lane all the way down to the junction **(Point A)**, to pick up the route beside the old airfield.

2. For a shorter circular walk, turn **left** along the track **(Point B)** to the right of the hedge and follow it down to some houses **(Point C)** where you turn left towards Market Farm, and you join the road through Tindon End.

If doing the shorter walk from Thaxted, and going through West Wood at **Point E**, turn **left** along the lane through Market Farm, passing **Point C** (where you also turn left) to the end of the next field **(Point B)**, where you turn **left** back to Thaxted.

62

Walk Eleven: 10 miles
Thaxted to Debden

Thaxted is a small town well served by shops, and its church had the highest spire in the county until Saffron Walden went a few feet higher. It is said that pilots landing at Stansted Airport use the spire as a navigational aid, and the reason for that suggestion will be obvious at times during this walk. Thaxted developed in the Middle Ages as a cutlery town and, as there were no mines nearby, most of the iron ore was brought up from Kent. Presumably, this was by water, and we can only assume that the River Chelmer formed the final leg of that raw materials journey. In 1381 at the time of the Black Death, there were 249 registered tradesmen in Thaxted, of whom 78 were cutlers and a further 17 had associated trades. It should be pointed out that in 1381 the cutler did not make knives and forks, but was most likely to be seen manufacturing a sword, shield or other item of war. The hamlet of Cutlers Green, whilst not being visited, is mentioned in the following commentary. The Friday market and most of the shops are in the main street, and you can stock up before the walk. Debden has its pub, a Nepalese restaurant and a community store, as well as an hourly weekday bus back to Thaxted. So whilst this is a longer walk, there are options to make it a leisurely all-day walk or a one-way walk. I have also outlined two short cuts, in case you find the whole walk a bit too long, also you are never far from the bus route. The walk starts at Thaxted Guildhall and will take a minimum of 4 hours to walk the 10 miles (5 miles each way). The walk is almost entirely on paths and tracks with only a couple of short stretches on very quiet lanes, the final stretch back to Thaxted being along Watling Lane. The link point if you are continuing on to Widdington is Debden School.

If starting from the Margaret Street car park (where public toilets are available), turn **right** out of the car park, and walk a few yards up the road, before turning **left** into Bell Lane, which comes out opposite the church. The shops and Guildhall **[1]** are down the hill, but our route goes up the hill towards *The Swan*. Cross the road and turn **left** through the little church car park to follow the path to a gap between the thatched and tiled single-storey cottages, and beside the churchyard extension to the windmill.

Walk 11: Thaxted to Debden

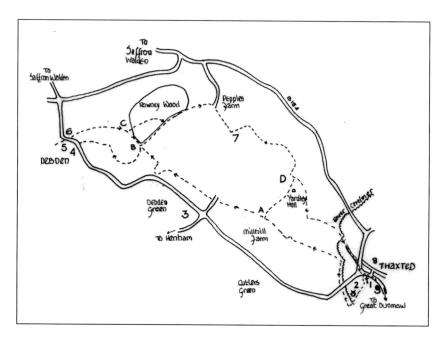

1. Thaxted Guildhall – START & FINISH
2. John Webb's Windmill
3. Bus stops
4. The *Plough* - Debden
5. Debden School – LINK POINT for Widdington
6. Debden Shop & car park
7. Broadoaks Manor
8. Thaxted car park
9. Thaxted shops

POINTS A, B, C & D - SHORTER WALK OPTIONS

John Webb's windmill **[2]** has recently been restored and is open to the public during the afternoon at weekends and bank holidays from May to September. Like most windmills, it is on high land and there is an opportunity to enjoy the view. Stay on the path to the next track, where you turn **right** beside the hedge down the hill to where it swings left and right to cross the River Chelmer. After crossing the river, turn **right** and follow it back to the road where there is a pumping station, Just before the road, there is a large converted barn on the other side if the river. As

64

Walk 11: Thaxted to Debden

you walk beside the river, what looks like an odd-looking tree to your left is actually a mobile telephone mast at Cutlers Green, known affectionately as an Orange Tree.

Cross the road and continue beside the river. You may be pondering how boats carrying iron ore managed to get up such a narrow river 600 years ago, but remember that all work was done by hand at that time and a tradesman would not require a great deal of raw material to keep him occupied for a long time. The boat would either be powered by sails or oars so would not be that large. Also man had not interfered with the landscape as much as he has now. The only river you will see larger than this one, in the whole of this book, is the Granta at Great Chesterford.

Stay beside the river, crossing a plank bridge and farm track to enter the second field, where the river meanders and occasionally leaves the path. At the end of the second field once again go through the hedge and then, at the point where the river swings to the right, continue across the field on the path to a track.

Turn **left** up the track, passing a red-brick house at which point the surface becomes grassy. After a couple of hundred yards, go through a break in the hedge on your **right**, then backtrack to the field-edge, before turning **left** up the hill towards a pylon. In spring, the ditch on your right may be covered with cowslips. Go under the pylon to the top of the field, where you turn **right** over a bridge and along the top of the next field, where there is a good view of Thaxted. Continue towards the hedge, where you turn **left** along a bridleway in the direction of the hidden Millhill Farm. If you are using an old Ordnance Survey map, don't get confused, as the pylons were moved a few years ago and some maps still show them following their old route. The radio mast at Henham and a water tower near Cutlers Green are clearly visible from here.

Another change from the map is that the path is shown as going between the two buildings, but it is now much easier to follow as you pass the grounds of both houses, crossing the drive before turning **right** on the wide grass track down the hill to the newly-landscaped grounds of Woodhams Farm. Upon reaching the bottom of the hill from Millhill Farm, turn **left** onto the main track **(Point A)** opposite the farm machinery, to a footbridge on the **right** about 150 yards along the drive beyond the new lake. Cross the bridge and stay in the same direction amongst the farm machinery, then over a track and two more single-

Walk 11: Thaxted to Debden

plank footbridges. This whole area was re-landscaped when the pond was developed, and has a very new and organised look about it.

There are now two large fields to cross. In the first field, aim for a tree towards the top and, when you reach it, the bridge out of the field is easy to find. The next field is much larger, and without the aid of a cleared path it is difficult to plot an accurate route. Initially, aim for a point between the two pylons (about one-third of the distance between the two from the right-hand pylon). When you reach the brow of the hill, you should see a waymark and a gate in the hedge, if not aim for the house in the trees to the left of the gabled house.

At the hedge, go through the small gate into an area of young trees, where there is a white seat just beyond the gate - take the central grass path forward to another small gate and a drive up towards Sibbards Farm, perhaps with some chickens welcoming you. Pass a converted barn on your right prior to reaching the road. Turn **left** at the road for a few yards, then turn **right** before the house onto a path, which becomes a good cross-field path at the end of the garden fence. This path takes you over a bridge to a byway near Debden Green.

To continue the walk into Debden, turn **left** for a few yards and, like the previous road, turn **right** before the house, staying on the field-edge path beside two fields to the next track. Here, for a change you turn **right** for about 75 yards, before turning **left** onto a good cross-field path towards the corner of Becks Wood at Tendrings Farm.

We now embark on a route round three sides of a square to get to the other side of the farm. So when you reach the wood, turn **left** onto the track beside a barn and a hedge. Just before the road, turn **right** over a bridge to the corner of the trees, where there is another right turn to take you to the rear of Tendrings Farm, where there is a line of beech trees and a pond. The houses of Debden have now become visible.

The path now turns **left** towards Rowney Wood. A few yards past the corner of the wood **(Point B)** and just before a useful bench, turn **left** and follow the hedge, keeping it to your right. After about a quarter-mile where the hedge is broken and there is a tall tree, cross the bridge at the waymark into the adjoining field and continue in the same direction, turning **right** at the next two corners.

After turning **right** at the second corner, continue straight on across the field up to the hedge in the distance (do not go towards the farm buildings). Turn **left** at the broken hedge, and go to the corner of the field, where there are fine views towards Henham in the south – here, cross into the adjoining field and aim towards the right of two small

66

trees ahead, where you cross the ditch and stay in the same direction up towards Deynes House.

Once in the field you need to turn **left** onto another cross-field path - it is usually reinstated, but if not then follow this route. A little more than halfway across the field towards Deynes Lane, line yourself up with the end of the hedge on your right, before heading left to the right of the second telegraph pole and a gabled brick bungalow and tall fence. At the fence there is a path between the houses to the road opposite the *Plough* **[4]**, where you turn **right** towards the school **[5]**, and village shop **[6]**, and bus stops.

RETURN ROUTE TO THAXTED

Deynes Road is beside the Yuva Resaurant and leads you to a surfaced footpath signposted to Deynes Farm and Deynes House. Progress to a narrow grass track and pass a hidden pond on the left. Keep the hedge to your left and head towards Rowney Wood, which is clearly visible ahead. A Forestry Commission sign (which now appears to have been removed) stated that this is part of Walden Forest and, as in most commercial woods in the area, the state of the tracks varies depending upon when tree felling was last carried out. At the end of the second field the path descends into the wood **(Point C)**, which is usually very quiet until a pheasant panics at the sound of your footsteps. The wood is also home to deer and rabbits as well as many species of birds.

Stay on the track over the first cross-track and continue some distance to the next crossing, where you turn **right** and then immediately take the **right** fork to a T-junction near the edge of the wood. Now turn **left** and follow this wide track. After a while the track veers right before turning to the **left** - at this point take the narrow path that continues straight on, then fork **left**. This path can get very muddy, so be careful as you ignore all the tracks that run from it, and it will take you to the corner of Rowney Wood and onto a wooded track. Pepples Farm can be seen to the right.

Stay on the track with its old trees until you reach the end of the second field on your **right**, where you cross a plank footbridge. Then follow the field-edge round, turning **left** then **right** at the corner of the field down to another footbridge. Turn **right** onto the lane towards Pepples Farm, where it turns **left** before becoming a byway just after Conyards Cottage, a thatched house with a pond.

Walk 11: Thaxted to Debden

Stay on the byway until it turns sharp **right**. Here you continue straight on along a footpath beside a couple of solitary trees, one of which is dead. There are extensive views from this field and if lucky, Thaxted Church spire can be seen. Much closer, however, is Broadoaks Manor **[7]**, a moated farmhouse built in 1570, and later featuring in the Gunpowder Plot. The Manor is now much smaller than it was in the 16th century, but the development of barns have caused it to be extended beyond the moat, which is now on only two sides of the site.

At the end of the field turn **left** towards the Manor and continue on to the left of the moat, before turning **right** in front of the house. Go between a barn and a pond on the track, and pass another two barns before following the clear path beside the wood. Cross the footbridge at the end of the wood, and keep to the **left** of the field down to the bottom and another bridge, which you cross and turn **left** beside the hedge to the corner, where there is an uncultivated area and a pond. Cross this area and a footbridge before turning **right**, follow the ditch to the end of the field where you cross another bridge and bear right staying beside the ditch towards a wood. About 200 yards before you get to the wood, turn **right** at a waymark post over a bridge and up the field edge, keeping the hedge to your left - you will notice Yardley Farm over to your left. At the top of the field, turn **left** towards a surfaced track **(Point D)**.

For Thaxted, turn **left** onto the track, keeping the woodland on your right, and at its end turn **right** along the diverted field-edge path, initially beside the wood; and then turn **left** and **right** in the same field as you descend to a concrete bridge over the River Chelmer - it is likely that you will be treading on deer tracks along this path.

Turn **left** after the bridge and **right** up a field-edge path on the left-hand side of the field into a woodland at the top, where there is a clear path to a field. Stay on the edge of this field as it winds its way down to the bottom, ignoring the bridge at the top, where you go through a gap and turn **left** towards the rebuilt, isolated bungalow called 'Haslemere'. You are now on a clear track back towards the river – cross this and walk beside it, until the track starts to climb and becomes a road called Watling Lane. This is a lane with

Walk 11: Thaxted to Debden

individual houses, so they are all detached in their own grounds and offer an opportunity to enjoy the views through the gaps as you climb.

The lane joins the main road at the church and there are places available for refreshments in the High Street. The Guildhall is on the main street on your right. For the car park **[8]** turn left down Bell Lane. There are shops including a tea shop **[9]** further down the main road.

SHORT CUTS

1. For a shorter walk back to Thaxted, turn **right** at **Point A** up the main track beside Woodhams Farm. Stay on the track until you turn **left** over a bridge; after passing a large open barn, climb gently beside Wain House and Yardley Hall, passing a wood on your right. to a right-hand bend **(Point D)**, from where you pick up the route back to Thaxted.

If walking to and from Debden, at **Point D** when joining the surfaced track, take the farm road immediately on your **right**, and follow this down to Yardley Hall. Keep the little cottage (Wain House) on you right and a couple of ponds on the left, down to a bridge where you turn **right** beside a large open barn, staying on the track which leads on towards Woodhams Farm. After passing the house, and before reaching the new lake and farm implements, the route from Thaxted comes in from the left at **Point A**.

2. For a walk back to Thaxted without visiting Debden, from **Point B** stay beside the wood on the wide verge until you reach the wide path coming in from the left, where you turn right into the woods **(Point C)**.

For a short circular walk back to Debden, do not go into the wood at **Point C**, but turn **right** beside it all the way down to the corner **(Point B)**, where you turn **right** again beside the hedge.

Walk 12: 4½ miles   Start TL556334
Debden To Widdington

This is one of the shorter routes in the book and will take about 2 hours to walk the 4½ miles (2 miles out and 2½ miles back). Widdington has a pub but no shops. There are no stiles on this route, but some of the cross-field paths are not always reinstated as quickly as they should be, and parts of the route may be muddy after rain. Both villages have hourly weekday bus services linking Saffron Walden and Bishop's Stortford, but there is no direct link between the two villages. The link point, if continuing on to Henham, is Widdington Church. The car park is at the playing fields near the school [2], and this is also the location of the community shop, and is close to the village's pub and restaurant.   Since the Yuva Nepalese Restaurant opened, the villages Debden and Wimbish have entered into a twinning arrangement with a Nepalese village, Tang Ting.

From the car park **[1]**, walk beside the pond to the school. In recent years, the pond has supported an increasing population of carp. From the school **[2]**, go down the hill towards the parish church **[3]**. The lane, with its ivy-covered banks, has a few houses separated by woodlands. The small church of St Mary the Virgin & All Saints, which is usually open, is at the bottom of the hill and has recently been expanded with the building of a new room on its north-eastern corner. The main building dates from the 13th century, the pillars either side of the nave being the oldest part.

After visiting the church, continue to its west end, then diagonally **right** to the kissing gate in the corner. On your left is a woodland, and on the right a very large brick building which spent its early life as stables. Turn **left** to the bridge over Debden Water, where you can observe the ducks, but if lucky may be rewarded by a glimpse of a kingfisher. The path then runs between fields to some woods. We walk through Cabbage Wood, an ancient woodland, where bluebells and dogs mercury flower in the

Walk 12: Debden to Widdington

spring. At the far end of the wood, on the right there is a disused single-storey building dated 1905, and to the left a barn. The waymarked cross-field path goes from the right of the barn to the right-hand corner of Park Wood ahead.

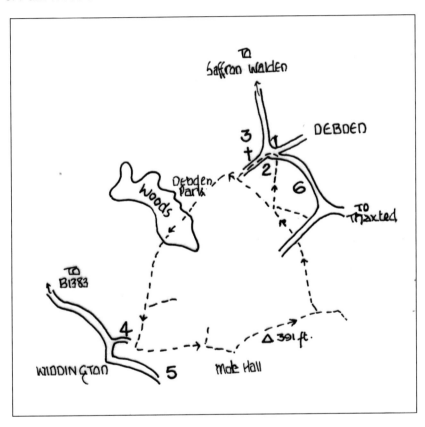

1. Village shop and car park
2. Debden School – START & FINISH
3. Debden Parish Church
4. Widdington Parish Church – LINK POINT for Henham
5. *Fleur de Lys* pub, Widdington
6. The *Plough* pub, Debden

Walk 12: Debden to Widdington

Keep Park Wood to your left until you enter the next field, where again there is a cross-field path in the same direction up the hill. About halfway up there is a waymark and the route becomes clear as you stay in the same direction towards the tall trees, which form the backs of gardens of Widdington houses. Turn **right** along the top of the field until the path turns **left** beside Widdington Church **[4]**. There is a seat under a tree on the little green.

The name Widdington comes either from the Saxon *Wid ing ton* ('situated among woods') or from *Wigegntun* (Willow Farm) and, like most place names, its spelling has changed dramatically over the centuries. In 1174 it was Widetone and 200 years later was called Wodeton; as recently as 1768 it was spelt with just one 'd'. To visit the pub or continue on to Henham, go down the hill to the larger green and keep **left** along the road where the *Fleur De Lys* pub **[5]** is on your left.

RETURN ROUTE TO DEBDEN

From the church **[4]**, take the little lane opposite, keeping the white house to your right. The road soon becomes a gravel drive and, when you reach the Black Barn, slip into the field on your **right** and stay in the same direction with the hedge on your left.

The path by the hedge adjoins the grounds of Widdington Hall, an estate dating back to the reign of Edward the Confessor. The Hall has changed hands several times, and at one time was owned by the Garnon family who had extensive property in the Stansted area and later changed their name to Montfitchet. Parts of the current building, which once had its own chapel, were built in the 15th century. A 16th century barn on the estate was demolished in 1937.

At the top of the hedge the path continues in the same direction across the field. It is not always easy to define the route of this cross-field path, so your first target is the telegraph pole and then, keeping in the same direction, go for the corner of the wood ahead.

Keep the trees and pond on your right as you pass Swaynes Hall, and stay on the track to the corner, just after a black, part-thatched barn, where you may find an ivy-clad bridleway sign pointing to your left. Swaynes Hall was one of seven farms in the area owned by King Henry VIII, but under the name Sweynes was also mentioned in 14th and 15th century documents. The current building and its timber-framed barn were erected in 1689.

72

Walk 12: Debden to Widdington

At one time hereabouts it was not unusual to hear the sound of animals from the nearby Mole Hall Wild Life Park, but the park closed in 2008. However, it is planned to re-open and is in process of reassembling its attractions, concentrating on British wildlife.

Follow the bridleway along the hedged track, where about halfway along some kind soul built a seat out of natural materials and even included a place to put your drinks containers. As the wood was not treated, its condition started to deteriorate after a few years. There is a new sign above the seat which reads 'seat made in 2006 by VWP – LN8 3TB' – this is a mystery, because the seat has been there much longer than that. And why would somebody in Lincolnshire plant a seat on a quiet Essex bridleway?

Stay on the track to the end and cross an opening where you will see Debden across the valley and Wimbish Barracks beyond. A nearby Trig Point here was sited at 391 feet above sea level, but these are now made redundant by new technology. Keep the hedge on your right as you wander through the next meadow, which in summer is covered in clover. At the far end, go through a gap in the hedge, so that it is now on your left, with large fields on your right. It can get a little muddy along here. At the corner, leave the field and follow the path as it goes into a small thicket, until you reach a track where you turn **left** down Sampson's Lane. A few years ago this byway was in very poor condition due to excess use by off-road vehicles, and it was safer to walk on the field-edge; it was subsequently closed and restored, but has deteriorated again.

Walk 12: Debden to Widdington

At the bottom of the track, cross the road towards the gate of the sewage works and turn **right** along its border beside a tributary to the River Granta. Turn **left** beside the fencing and fir trees, then up the hill, keeping to the left of the hedge towards Brocton's Plantation, one of many woods in the area which house pheasants. Keep to the right of the plantation and the left of the hedge, towards the school where you come out on the road. Turn **left** for the village shop and car park, or turn **right** for the *Plough* pub **[6]**. The bus stop for Saffron Walden is nearby on this side of the road.

Walk Thirteen: 7 miles
Widdington to Henham

Start TL539317

Widdington is a small village at the top of a hill above the old London to Newmarket road. It has a church, a pub and historic barn. Mole Hall Wildlife Park closed in 2008, but there are plans to re-open it. There is an hourly weekday bus service linking Bishop's Stortford and Saffron Walden, which stops at the village hall. Allow a minimum of 3 hours for this 7-mile walk (2½ miles out and 4½ miles back), which passes the pub in Henham and its community shop. There are two shorter walk options. The link point, if continuing on to Broxted, is Henham Stores. Whilst in Widdington, it is worth visiting the medieval Tithe Barn at Prior Hall, cared for by English Heritage, one of the best examples of such a building in England, over 500 years old, reached from the church by walking down to the green, then turning right along the road for about 300 yards until you reach the barn on your left. The Hall was owned by the same family for 850 years after the Norman Conquest, and could be one of Britain's oldest established houses.

From the church [1] walk down the hill to South Green, then **left** up beside some cottages to the High Street, which passes the village hall, village sign and the *Fleur de Lys* pub [2]. Stay on the road, which becomes Wood End, and go past the larger houses towards a seat beside the road, placed to commemorate the beginning and end of a resident's favourite walk.

75

Walk 13: Widdington to Henham

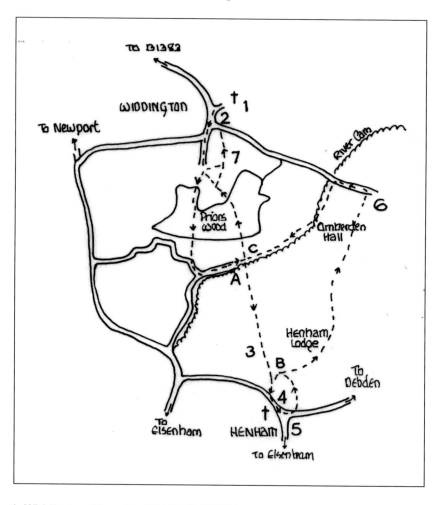

1. Widdington Church – START & FINISH
2. *Fleur de Lys* pub, Widdington
3. Fishing lakes
4. The *Cock* pub, Henham
5. Henham Stores – Link Point for Broxted
6. Lake at Amberden Hall
7. Newlands Farm

POINTS A, B, C SHORTER WALK OPTIONS

Walk 13: Widdington to Henham

In front of you is the impressive looking Widdington House, site of Birds Farm demolished in 1845, rebuilt as Aberystwyth House before changing its name to Widdington House. Turn **right** here for a few yards, and then **left** along a footpath between a fence and a hedge. At the end of the garden, where there are some fenced paddocks, cut across to the **right** over the meadow to enter Priors Wood, then follow the path just inside the wood. When you come to a junction of paths continue forward, taking the **left** option shown on the waymark post - this takes you through High Wood.

These woods are home to a herd of fallow deer, regularly seen from the nearby railway, and also to many species of birds, including greater spotted woodpeckers and owls. At the far side of the wood, go over the ditch into the field with a pond on your left. Cross this field to the left of the hedge, and follow it round to the very quiet lane serving Little Henham. Turn **left** down the lane for a couple of hundred yards until you reach a no-through road on your left.

Turn **left** again here along the lane. The tiny stream on your right is a very young River Cam (or Granta), which rises a couple of miles away on the other side of Amberden Farm. At the end of the surfaced road, continue on through the fencing to the byway, after a short distance turn **right** over a bridge and stile. **(Point A)**. Climb up the meadow to the gate and pylon at the top and into the next field. The map here shows the path going to the left of the hedge ahead, but in the past there have been problems leaving this field. So it is recommended that you use the route the locals take, which is to cross into the right-hand field and keep the hedge on your left all the way to the fishing lake. (The toilet here is for the exclusive use of the fishermen.) If you look to the top of the hill, Henham Church comes into view. Continue down to the lake **[3]**, then keep the hedge and ditch on your right beside the lake until you reach another track.

If you want a shorter walk avoiding the village, turn **left** here up to Henham Lodge and pick up the return route at **(Point B)**. Our route turns **right** over the bridge up to the road where you go **left** towards the church and the *Cock* pub **[4]** opposite. The village duck ponds are a little further on opposite the road junction. The community shop **[5]** is on the right opposite these ponds.

Walk 13: Widdington to Henham

RETURN ROUTE TO WIDDINGTON

Like Widdington, Henham is also a hilltop village but it has managed to maintain more facilities. The large old building on the junction is the old school but, unlike many, when this one closed a new larger school was opened on the edge of the village. Henham also has good sports facilities including a tennis club. The ponds and wide greens give the impression of a spacious village.

From the shop **[5]** cross the road to walk beside another pond until you reach the hidden damaged old pump near a willow tree. Turn **left** along the footpath before Clematis Cottage, and follow it with the hedge on your left beside the fields down to the track **(Point B)**. Here, turn **right** up to Henham Lodge, where, in the meadows on the right you may spot llamas. In the early 17th century, Henham Lodge, then a moated farmhouse, was said to be the home of the Henham Dragon, pictured on the village sign near the start of the walk, which allegedly would sun itself on the edge of nearby Birch Wood.

At the old pump, turn **left** beside the recently-converted barns, then turn **right** behind their gardens towards an older house and greenhouse, before returning to open countryside. There is now a clear path passing a small wood, then going under a couple of lines of electricity cables as it climbs, falls and rises again, finally becoming a track beside a hedge

78

up to Amberden Hall. After passing the farm buildings, you drop down to a lane, before which is a large lake **[6]** and on your left is an area housing ducks and chickens.

At the lane, turn **left** beside a lightly-wooded area where the bank is covered in the spring with snowdrops and aconites. Continue on until you reach a white house called Churchfield Cottage on your right – opposite this is a gate and a track (path 37) which you follow up beside a newly-planted hedge called Handa's Hedgerow. At the top where the track turns left, you need to leave it and continue forward with the hedge initially on your left as it works its way through a couple of fields down to and then beside the River Granta with trees now to your right.

At the end of the field, cross the bridge and follow the infant river downstream, enjoying a pleasant walk along this path which, even though it is regularly restored, is still subject to erosion. For several years, there has been a leaning oak obstructing the path but there is a path round it. Soon after this, go through a gap in the hedge on the **right (Point C)**. (If you reach a bridge on your left, you have gone about 20 yards too far.) Go along a cross-field path to Priors Wood. Enter the wood by a gate that has been falling apart for years, or do as most people appear to do and cross the ditch. There is a clearly-defined track through the wood, but watch your feet as it can be very wet and uneven. Whilst walking through here, I once watched a woodpecker above me pecking at a tree, and have often seen deer or muntjac running across the path ahead.

At the top, the track turns **left**, then bears **right** before you see a hand-built type of kissing gate on your right beside a waymark. Do not leave the track here, but continue along a little further to the next similar structure and go through this one before heading towards a gap in the hedge where a tennis court can be seen. Turn **right** and walk round the tennis court, and towards an isolated kissing gate and cattle trough in the middle of the field, then on to another modified kissing gate to the left of a greenhouse. The path now runs through a lightly-wooded area beside a garden until it reaches a gate, where you turn **right** along the drive towards Newlands Farm **[7]**.

Before reaching the first building, turn **left** and go through a farm gate into a meadow, and follow the pond to the far side where, at the left-hand corner, there is a bridge and gate. Go **left** through the gate (which is not waymarked) and follow the path onto a fenced path which adjoins the garden of a large house. Parts of this path can be muddy but stay on it until you reach Cornells Lane, where you turn **left**. Before this,

Walk 13: Widdington to Henham

take a look at the footpath sign - not only does it say 'Parish of Widdington' on the upright, but the faded pointer states the distance to Henham. At the end of the lane, turn **right** for the pub, village green and church.

SHORT CUT OPTIONS

1. At **Point A**, stay on the track for another 20 yards or so, and take the path on your left **(Point C)** up to Priors Wood. If walking from Henham and wishing to avoid Widdingon, stay on the path at **Point C** and cross the bridge on your left at **Point A**.

2. To avoid Henham, turn **left** at **Point B** and continue the walk from **Point B** in the return route (which is the same place).

Walk Fourteen: 7 miles   Start TL547274
Henham to Broxted

Henham (meaning 'high dwelling') is a small village noted for its ponds and wide greens beside the roads. It has a pub opposite the church, and a small village community shop which is open six days a week and Sunday mornings. It also has an hourly bus service serving Elsenham, Stansted and the airport. However there is no direct bus link with Broxted. The walk starts at Henham Village Stores opposite the ponds, and will take a minimum of 2¾ hours to walk the 7 miles (3½ miles each way). There are no facilities in Broxted (the *Prince of Wales* pub is off the route). Broxted is served by the hourly bus service 5 which also serves Thaxted and the airport. There are no short cuts on this walk, with most of the paths being on the edges of fields. Both Chickney and Broxted Churches are well worth visiting and the link point, if continuing on to Elsenham, is at the junction at the top of the path from Broxted Church. The close proximity to the airport will be apparent during much of this walk, but in spite of that you will still feel moments of beauty, peace and tranquillity, especially in Hawland Wood and the two churches passed on the route.

Our walk starts at the community shop **[1]**, opposite the duck ponds, just after the junction of the road to Elsenham and Thaxted. From here, follow the road towards Debden, passing the ponds with mallard and moorhen swimming in all weathers. Go beside a wide green on the right with the site of Starr Garage behind it. *The Starr* was once one of the four pubs in Henham. According to the Session Rolls of 1792, there were several weavers, farmers, labourers and paupers in the parish, but only two 'Gentlemen' and one tradesman (a fan maker) - four years later it was described as a 'dull neighbourhood', but it seems lively enough now!

Walk 14: Henham to Broxted

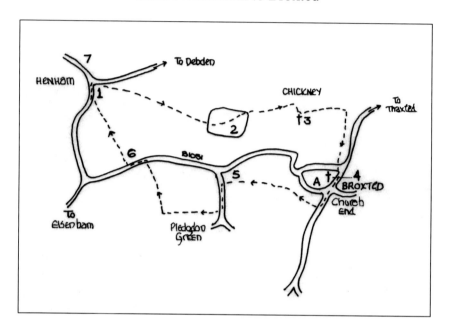

1. Henham Shop – START & FINISH
2. Hawland Wood
3. Chickney Church
4. Broxted Church
5. LINK POINT FOR ELSENHAM
6. Palegates Farm
7. Pledgdon Hall
8. The *Cock* pub at Henham

Continue along a little further before turning **right** into Hall Close, a private road with modern houses on the left. After passing number three, turn **left** between the fences and over a footbridge, before entering a field where the re-routed path borders it. Turn **right** at the first corner and keep the hedge to your left, until you meet a cross-field path coming in from the right. Here, turn **left** beside a couple of paddocks with notices asking you not to feed the horses. You then cross a footbridge before turning **right** along another private road opposite Holmwood, towards Grind Hall and Green End.

Walk 14: Henham to Broxted

The road twists to the left of an occasional pond bordered by trees, the largest of which is a sycamore, before straightening out again on its way to Green End Farm, which dates from the 16th century. Just before the farm, take the grass path on the left beside a conifer hedge, turning **right** at the corner before dropping down to a ditch at the bottom of the field. Cross the ditch and continue up between the two open fields to a hedge.

Hawland Wood **[2]** is ahead and, to enter it, walk to the left of the hedge where, just after reaching the wood, there is a path on your **right**. This is a delightful wood and, even though as you approach, it looks as though there are low-flying aircraft above, once in the wood this appears not to be the case (in fact they fly over Chickney Church). This ancient wood shows signs of coppicing and in spring there is a good selection of flowers, while autumn provides a carpet of leaves to walk on. Alas, this peaceful interlude soon comes to an end as you leave the wood and turn **right** beside it along a wide track, down towards a small car park (for a shooting club) and Chickney Lane, which is no more than a surfaced track - turn **right** up to a farm and a drive, then **left** to Chickney Church **[3]**. Take the short diversion into the churchyard and visit the church, which is now in the care of The Churches Conservation Trust and usually open. The interior is simple, lit by a candle chandelier  as there is no electricity here and there have not been regular services since the late 19th century, when the parish was absorbed into the much larger parish of Broxted. but occasional services continue to be held in summer.

After your visit, return to the drive and go through the gates of New Chickney Hall, before veering **left** over a stile into a meadow. Cross the meadow and leave over another stile on the opposite side, before turning **right** then **left** at the end of the hedge. Stay on the field edge, above the buildings, which include a barn conversion and an attractive little garden with a horse trough feature. Continue on to cross a stile and a ditch where it can be a little damp. Now cross the meadow to the next stile and bridge, then within a few yards to a second stile (which may have collapsed). Cross the broken fence and aim for the

Walk 14: Henham to Broxted

right of the meadow, to climb steeply up to the next stile in the corner (a tall one and also in poor condition).

You may notice two other walk waymarks at some of the recent stiles. The Five Parishes Millennium Walk was created in the year 2000 to celebrate the united church parishes of Chickney, Broxted, Tilty and Great and Little Easton. The Saffron Trail is a long distance route from Prittlewell (near Southend) to Saffron Walden.

Keep beside the fence on your right, and at the corner follow it round to the **right** beside horse chestnut trees (this section is not waymarked), and onto a track towards a gate. Just before the gate, there is a farm track on which you turn **left**, keeping the farm buildings of Chaureth (meaning Cherry) Hall Farm to your right. Immediately after passing the final building and at the end of the fencing on the right, turn

right up to a newly-built barn. At the rear end of the barn, turn **left** across the field and aim for the bridge in the hedge at the bottom - this is in line with the white house at the top of the next hill. This path is not always cleared.

Cross the bridge over one of the tributaries of the River Chelmer, then climb up the new field, initially towards the spire of Broxted Church. The White House once again comes into view, and you leave the field in front of this building. Don't forget to look behind you as you climb to get one last glance of Chickney Church spire above the trees.

Whitehall is now a very nice hotel and restaurant, but previously it was the home of R. A.('Rab') Butler who was Member of Parliament for the Saffron Walden constituency from 1929 to the 1960s, and served in the Cabinet for many years. He was also the last man to be buried in the churchyard in Saffron Walden.

Turn **right** along the road for a few yards before turning **left** up the track to St Mary's Church, Broxted **[4]**. This is another church well worth visiting, particularly to see the 'Hostage Window' at the west end, which depicts the grey gloom of John McCarthy (who had local connections) when he was held hostage in Lebanon and the joy of freedom following his release.

Walk 14: Henham to Broxted

Broxted is reached by returning to the path and climbing beside the churchyard and a fenced path to a road junction **(Point A)**. You may decide at this point to walk on to Elsenham or Stansted where you can get the hourly weekday bus Route 7 back to Henham.

RETURN ROUTE TO HENHAM

The route back is much more direct, initially beside fields and finishing along a good track. After leaving the church you climb up to a junction, where you turn **right** along the road passing two large houses the size of which suggests that the village was once more important: they are the large 'Old Post Office' and the even more prominent 'Old Vicarage'. The house between them is Brick House but Brick End is elsewhere in Broxted - you are currently in Church End. Turn **left** opposite the Old Vicarage where there is a seat. The signpost here points towards Takeley and Broxted!

On the left is Cranham Road where there is a Queen's Jubilee celebration post erected in 2002. On the **right** before the terraced houses (School Villas) is a footpath - follow this through two gates and keep to the right in the meadow, before turning **left** at the next corner where you continue through a kissing gate and over a bridge into a huge field.

Turn **right** in the field keeping the hedge to your right until a point where it turns **right** - here the map shows the path leaving the hedge to cross the field, but there is a perfectly good field-edge path if the correct route has not been cleared, in fact the waymark appears to favour the field-edge route. Along this stretch I have seen the remains of tree houses and even footballs, but no signs of civilisation. When the hedge finally turns right for a second time at a waymark, you need to continue straight across the field towards the posts of a bridge. Cross the bridge into a small field and cross a stile into the grounds of Palegates Farm **[5]**.

Walk on the concrete path across the main drive and through an iron gate into an area beside a barn, which can be packed with all kinds of machinery, garden supplies and vehicles. Be very careful as you plot your route through this area, keeping the barn to your left. This part of the route is well waymarked and once through you will soon find a stile and a bridge to cross. The adventure may not quite be over unless the next path has been reinstated, as you now need to cross this field to a

85

Walk 14: Henham to Broxted

point on the road to the left of a clump of trees. Turn **left** at the road towards Pledgdon Green. I remember walking into the village on one occasion and reading a notice on the pillar box which stated that to improve the postal service the last collection from the box would in future be at 9 a.m. – improve it for whom, I wondered?

Before the 20 mph sign on the bend and first house on the right, turn **right** at footpath sign partly hidden by vegetation, cross an equally overgrown stile and walk beside the hedge until it turns. The map shows the path staying in the same direction to the trees and pond in the middle of the field, where you keep to the left before picking up a path between two open fields back to the quarry edge. However you may choose to keep to the field edge with the fence on your left, which would be a lot easier. The quarry has been responsible for several path diversions in this area of late, and it looks as though there is now a path beside the hedge from the road to this point.

Keep to the right of the quarry, until the border fence turns left - here you stay on the track away from the quarry towards some trees, which are to the left of the footpath. You will soon reach the B1051 road, which can seem like a race track, and the verge may also be a bit difficult for walking. However, after turning **left**, we are only on the road for a few minutes as we pass Pledgdon Hall **[6]** which, like Whitehall further up this road, is popular for weddings and conferences. There has been a building on the site of Pledgdon Hall since Norman times and the present building dates back to the 17th century.

After passing the hall, turn **right** along the track signposted to The Barn car park and Saplings Nursery. If you were planning to buy a tree at the nursery, you will be disappointed when you see the brightly-coloured plastic toys adorning the bungalow! Stay on this track, passing the playing fields and buildings of Henham & Ugley School on your left. After the school at the corner of the field, turn **left** onto a lane and beside some houses and the tennis club, to the church hall and the greens. Turn **right** on the greens past the old Board School and the war memorial at the junction, and so back to the start. For the *Cock* pub **[7]**, turn **left** at the junction.

Walk 15: 8¼ miles
Broxted to Elsenham

Start TL578271

Broxted is a scattered parish with several areas of settlement - this walk starts at Church End, the link point being outside the Old Post Office. The pub at Broxted is not passed on this walk as it is at Brick End. The village has an hourly weekday bus service linking Saffron Walden with Bishop's Stortford, serving Thaxted and the airport. Whilst Elsenham also has an hourly service, to get between the two villages you would have to change at the airport. There is limited parking in the Church End area. The walk starts at the Old Post Office and will take about 4 hours to cover the 8¼ miles (3½ miles out and 4¾ miles back). Elsenham has a shop, take-away and pub, as well as train and bus services. It may be easier to start this walk at Elsenham as there are more parking options. There is a shorter option which will roughly halve the length of the walk. The paths are generally good and there is some road walking in the Broxted area. The link point, if continuing to Stansted, is the village shop in Elsenham.

From the Old Post Office **[1]**, keep the large houses on your right as you pass Brick House and the Old Vicarage. See Walk 14 for description of Broxted Church **[2]**. Opposite the Old Vicarage is a road signposted Broxted (!), and Takeley. Take this road and walk past a couple of paddocks and Cranham Road, with the Queen's Jubilee sign on the corner. Continue on the road beside School Villas, and turn **right** after the final cottage. Stay in the same field to the left of the hedge as it turns right then left at a junction of paths. Walk beside the hedge until it is no more, then continue in the same direction on a good cross-field path all the way across a large open field into the next field, with this hedge once again to your right.

Follow this hedge round the field as it zig-zags, ignoring the two bridges on your right, and keeping to the edge until you reach a kissing gate. At this point there is a note stating that the path has been diverted. Go through both kissing gates to the road. You are now at the southern end of the hamlet of Pledgdon Green - to divert to see the large village green, turn right. The route to Elsenham involves turning **left** onto the road and passing Wood Farm, just after the next drive on the right, there is a slightly hidden footpath sign that takes us behind a large bungalow to the corner of the field. Ignore the bridge here and turn **right** beside the same field, keeping the hedge to your left.

87

Walk 15: Broxted to Elsenham

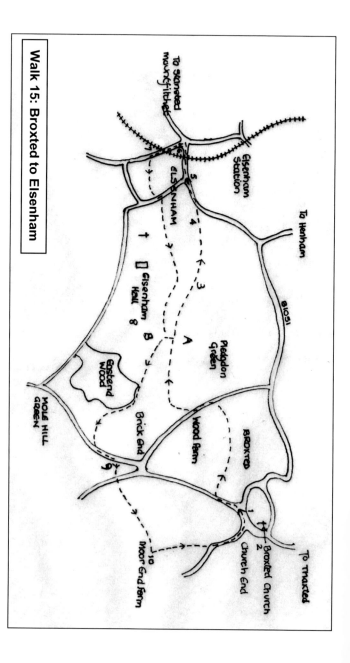

1. **Broxted Church End - START & FINISH**
2. **Broxted Church**
3. **Lady Wood**
4. **Elsenham Golf Course & driving range**
5. *Crown Inn*, Elsenham

6. **Shops & LINK POINT**
7. **Railway Crossing – *TAKE CARE!***
8. **Home Farm**
9. **Garrolds**
10. **Moor End Farm**

POINTS A & B SHORTER WALK OPTIONS

Walk 15: Broxted to Elsenham

As you walk along here you will notice a new house on the other side of the field - amazingly, this house was built *after* news of a potential second runway at the airport was announced – you will notice how low the aircraft are at this point. Among the trees before crossing the bridge, there has been a heap of broken glass for several years - more of a hazard to wildlife than walkers. Stay in the same direction along a narrow hedged path beside two large meadows. At the end, cross the footbridge on your **left** before continuing in the same direction, with Pledgdon Wood on your right. The wood appears to have been managed at some time, as there are many signs of coppicing. There is another bridge on the right at the corner of the next field, which needs to be crossed to continue to Elsenham **(Point A)**. However, for the shorter route back to Broxted, turn **left** before the bridge to the track on the other side of the field, where you turn **left** again.

After crossing the bridge, turn **left** towards Lady Wood **[3]** where you stay on the diverted path between the wood and the golf course **[4]** and driving range. At the end of the woods is a quarry road - be careful as you cross it, stay on path 19 and go down some steps onto a wooded path and cross a bridge. Then climb gently towards a house and the main Elsenham to Thaxted road. Turn **left** along the pavement beside the impressive 16th century timber-framed house called Elsenham Place. This house used to be in the parish of Henham when it was simply called Place Farm. Stay on the road with the meadow on your left, until you reach the *Crown Inn* **[5]** at the junction. The shops **[6]** are a couple of hundred yards further along on the left.

Walk 15: Broxted to Elsenham

RETURN ROUTE TO BROXTED

From the *Crown* in Elsenham, continue along the road towards the village centre, passing the school and pump with shelter. The shops soon appear on your left **[6]**, after which you turn **left** down Robin Hood Road - the old pub, which closed in 1988, can still be  identified about halfway down on the left. After passing Rush Lane on the right, you reach the railway. When the line to Cambridge was first built this was the site of the station, but the gradient was too steep so it was moved to its current position. Queen Victoria passed this way in 1847 on her way by train to Cambridge.

There is a light-controlled pedestrian crossing here, so *cross with care* and obey the lights **[7]**. Only about one in three trains passing here stop at Elsenham, and the others can be travelling anything up to 70 mph as they pass this spot. After crossing the railway lines, stay on the road beside an industrial estate until you take the footpath on the **left**, just before the road turns slightly to the right by the telegraph pole.

Cross the bridge and go through the gate, before climbing a stile into a paddock, where you go diagonally across to the bottom corner. After crossing this stile, walk beside the stream for a few yards as far as the bridge. Do not cross this bridge, but take the stile to your **right** into a meadow which you cross diagonally and aim for a point about two-thirds of the way along the hedge from your left on the opposite side of the meadow. Cross the stiles between the two meadows, and now walk towards the right-hand corner and the road. Cross the road and turn **left** onto the footway down the hill for about 50 yards where you turn **right** onto a bridleway into the woods. (If you wanted to take a more direct shorter route, but don't mind walking near fast-moving traffic, this bridleway can be reached by taking the road opposite the pub towards Takeley.)

Elsenham Church, where records date back to 1070, appears through the trees to your right and, like many village churches, is on the Hall estate as distinct from the village. In Elsenham several Sunday services are held in the village hall to save the long trek out here. Elsenham Hall's most famous owner was Sir Walter Gilbey who made his money in East London distilling gin. Edward VII, whilst still the Prince of Wales, regularly visited the Hall whilst he was staying with Lady

Walk 15: Broxted to Elsenham

Warwick at Easton Lodge. Elsenham Hall was also the original home of the Elsenham Jam Company, which started in 1891 making jam from the surplus fruit produced in the kitchen gardens of the Hall.

The path through the wood is easy to follow, the only difficulty being that it is also a bridleway and horses have churned up the soft woodland soil in some places. The path climbs steadily and continues in an attractive wooded area before reaching open land. Cross the surfaced track to a diverted path on the golf course, which runs to your left at about 45 degrees, over a ditch and then to the left of the hedge. The right-of-way is beside the hedge and goes near the golf course, so take care. Just after the 18th ladies' tee, cross back over the ditch and leave the golf course with the hedge now on your left.

You can see Home Farm **[8]** at the top of the hill on your right as you head east along a good path. Turn **left** with the path when there is a gate in front of you, and when you reach a path coming in from your left **(Point B)**, continue forward. Your route soon becomes an attractive hedged path towards East End Wood.

As you approach East End Wood the track narrows and when it turns right, leave the bridleway and take the footpath which heads slightly to your left to enter a field. Keep the ditch and attractive wood to your right. This wood appears to have been left to its own devices recently and there are several fallen trees, but this gives it a natural feel. At the corner of the wood, go into the next field but stay beside the wood (the waymark seems to be at the wrong angle), as the route turns right and then left and right again, to the next field-corner, where you turn **left** to leave the woods. Just before next corner, turn **right** over the ditch, then immediately **left** over a plank bridge into the next field which, with the hedge on your left, leads you to a short hedged path and the lane at Molehill Green opposite Woodgates Farm.

Turn **left** along the lane, with Water Hall on your right and the remains of a pump opposite, past the byway (which is in such poor condition it could be dangerous for walkers). Carry on to Garrolds **[9]** where, after the pond and entrance drive, take the footpath on your **right** over a plank bridge to enter the field, keeping the buildings to your right. After passing the last barn, go through the gap, so that the hedge is now on your left and this will take you to the next road. The next path is found almost opposite, just beyond the Brick End sign. You are only about 100 meters above sea level, but there are excellent views from this path, including the village of Great Easton ahead and slightly to the right, and if you look to the left you will see your destination.

91

Walk 15: Broxted to Elsenham

Stay on this path and cross a bridge into the next field. When you reach a ditch at the end of the second field and Moor End Farm **[10]**, veer slightly **right** to follow the ditch towards an old barn where you meet a track. Turn **left** to cross the ditch and then climb behind the farm buildings, passing a couple of silos to your right. The path continues to climb up to a telegraph pole, before dropping down between two fields. Thaxted Church spire comes into view ahead to your right. Cross both of the bridges, and then turn slightly to your **right** as you climb up to a waymark and some trees in the garden of the right-hand cottage. Keep to the left of the fence, then to the right of the garage on to a drive to the road, where you turn **left** back to Broxted.

SHORT CUT OPTIONS

At **Point A** turn **left** instead of going over the bridge and follow the edge of the field to the track at the next corner **(Point B)**, where you turn **left** again towards the wood.

If walking from Elsenham, turn **left** into the field **(Point B)**, and walk along its edge to the next corner **(Point A)** and cross the bridge.

92

Walk 16: 6 miles
Elsenham to Stansted

Start TL534263

If you have walked the full Uttlesford Way, this will be the final stage, unless you are going to make it a six-day walk and go back the other way using the routes in the second half of each chapter. This walk starts at the small shopping parade in Elsenham, but do not park there as there is only limited space and it is for shoppers. It will take a minimum of 2½ hours to complete the 6 mile walk (2½ miles out and 3½ miles back). There are no short cuts, but there is a direct bus and train service between the two villages. Stansted is very well served with shops, pubs and eating places. The paths and tracks are good and there is some walking beside a busy road at the beginning of the return leg. Whilst you are very near the airport, the noise of the motorway is more noticeable, but it does not stop you enjoying a beautiful wood and dramatic valley encountered on the return journey. If you are continuing on to Manuden, the link point is the station.

The walk starts at the shops **[1]** and there is limited street parking nearby. Alternatively, the buses stop near the start of the walk, and the station **[2]** is about half-a-mile away. Walk along the High Street, keeping the shops to your right, then over the railway bridge before passing the site of the village pump, the shelter of which was donated by Sir Walter Gilbey in 1896 in memory of his wife. The Gilbeys moved

out to Elsenham Hall from East London and purchased the property with the money generated from the distillation of gin.

Elsenham was originally a clearing in the valley of Stansted Brook enclosed by the Forest of Essex, and was still such at the time of the Domesday Book when it was known as *Alsenham*. The forest, which extended as far south as the area now known as Waltham Forest, was used by royalty for hunting and was large enough to support over 3,500 swine.

93

Walk 16: Elsenham to Stansted

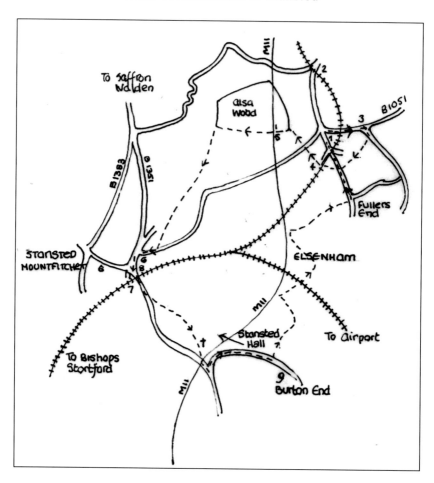

1. Elsenham shops – START & FINISH
2. Elsenham railway station
3. The *Crown* pub, Elsenham
4. Railway crossing – ___TAKE CARE!___
5. Bridge over motorway
6. Stansted Mountfitchet – shops, cafes & pubs
7. Stansted Mountfitchet railway station
8. Stansted Mountfitchet Castle
9. The *Ash*, Burton End

Walk 16: Elsenham to Stansted

You now go beside the garage and school, before turning **right** opposite the *Crown* **[3]** at Elsenham Cross, where there are several older premises including a former village shop. The Gilbey Memorial and the pub are both listed buildings. Walk down the road beside Camellia Cottage and Sophia Cottage along Hall Road. Stay on the pavement until just after The Old Vicarage Cottage, where there is a stile on the **right**. Climb this stile and then go into a meadow, staying along the top beside the bushes, before going through a kissing gate on the far side, where you turn **left** down to cross a footbridge. Here, the path turns right briefly beside the stream, before turning away to another stile.

This area is very popular horse country which is the reason for the meadows but, as horses tend to like to stand beside fences, sometimes the paths can be muddy or very uneven. Cross this meadow to a stile about halfway up the fence on the opposite side - this takes you along a narrow hedged track to a gate and a lane.

Turn **right** down the lane to the railway, where there are audible pedestrian lights to indicate whether it is safe to cross **[4]**. DO NOT CROSS IF THEY ARE RED, as not all trains stop at Elsenham Station and could well be travelling in excess of 70 mph at this point. If you do not wish to cross the railway, there is an alternative route outlined in a following paragraph.

This crossing was the original site of Elsenham Station, but the gradient towards Cambridge was so steep that it was difficult for some trains to get the necessary traction to restart after calling at the station, so it was moved to its present location. In 1896 a light railway branch line was opened to Thaxted at a cost of £30,000, but the plans to extend it to Finchingfield never materialised. It was later converted to standard gauge and between three and five trains ran daily. It was closed to passengers in 1952 and finally closed in 1957. The road also used to cross the railway here but, as it was so lightly used the crossing was closed several years ago.

Climb the road opposite to Rush Lane (If you wanted a short route you could have come down Robin Hood Road to this point where you would turn right, which also avoids the railway crossing). Robin Hood Road gets its name from a now-closed pub of that name which used to be on the right between Rush Lane and the shops. Turn **left** into Rush Lane which has houses only on the right. At the end, turn **right** onto the field-edge path which follows the edge of the housing up to Stansted Road. The population of the village increased from 720 in

95

Walk 16: Elsenham to Stansted

1951 to 1,705 in 1979, and if you look to your right after crossing the road you will see the reason.

Cross the road and enter the grassy open space opposite. Walk as far as a seat and from here you follow the surfaced area to the left until you reach a high fence, which will probably have cars behind it. Turn **right** here for a few yards until you reach a waymark post, with an arrow pointing **left** through a gap into Alsa Wood. Enter the wood and follow the path as it turns to the **left** towards the noise of the motorway.

Alsa Wood is an attractive area and has a special landscape value, with many trees in this SSSI subject to Tree Preservation Orders. However, this did not stop the planners carving a motorway through it. Now the constant drone of traffic takes away any peace. The path up to the motorway is the only path in the woods, all the rest are along its borders. The larger part of the wood to the west of the motorway does house foxes and plenty of bird life which can be seen from its edge.

Follow the path round to a bridge and cross over the motorway **[5]**, before descending to the track beside the wood as far as Keepers Cottage, which is after passing a track coming in from the left. At the cottage, turn **left** along another woodland edge path. This wood is part of the Aubrey Buxton Nature Reserve and is administered by the Essex Wildlife Trust. The landscape falls steeply away on the edge of the wood, suggesting that there may once have been a moat there. You may also notice Wildside Walk waymark signs.

Unfortunately, the next waymark sign is hidden in the bushes where the woodland edge turns sharp right, just after a short piece of fencing. Leave the track by continuing in the same direction as you have been walking, to cross the field to its corner about halfway along the trees ahead of you. This path is usually reinstated after ploughing so it should not cause a problem.

At the corner, turn **left** between the hedge and fence, as the (occasionally muddy) path makes its way out into another field, with a small corrugated iron and wooden barn on your right. Once again, go diagonally across this field where, looking right, the long distance walkers may recognise some of the landmarks they saw two days earlier, the new Roman Catholic Church being the most prominent building.

At the corner of the field, slip down the path beside the fence to some houses at Gall End. Turn **left** up beside a couple of cottages and a vegetable garden, staying on the grass path, keeping the hedge close on your left - this is a lovely piece of open space where rabbits enjoy life

96

Walk 16: Elsenham to Stansted

bobbing about. Once on top, where there is a telegraph pole in a clearing, aim to the left towards the chimneys of a house, but not towards the pond on the main path. Here, there is a path leading to a drive, which will bring you out onto Grove Hill, where you turn **right** down the hill to the village of Stansted Mountfitchet.

If you have been on the full walk, congratulations! You have now completed the Uttlesford Way - unless you plan to go back in the opposite direction, in which case you will need to follow the second half of each section, starting with this one and making your way back to section one. There is accommodation available in the village.

STANSTED MOUNTFITCHET

Stansted Mountfitchet is the largest community visited on the walk and has many facilities, including a station at the bottom of the village and further shops and pubs at the top **[6]**. There are several cafes along Lower Street, and there are a couple of pubs and 'take-aways in the arcade and towards the station **[7]**.. The village also has tourist attractions in the shape of a castle **[8]** and toy museum adjoining the main car park before the junction. So you can linger here for a while before returning to Elsenham. The two villages are linked by an hourly weekday bus service and an (at least) hourly train service, but by returning that way you will miss some amazing countryside, despite the fact that we are so close to a motorway and an international airport.

RETURN ROUTE TO ELSENHAM

From the station entrance **[7]**, walk along the approach road, passing some take-aways, to the crossroads, where you turn **right** beside the Lotus car dealership and over the railway (on the circular walk this is a left turn at the crossroads after the car park entrance). Stay on the pavement, passing Elms Farm, and continue as far as Churchfields. Immediately after this, take the tarmac track on the **left** beside some single-storey buildings, up to a large gate and a seat where the path runs to the left of

97

Walk 16: Elsenham to Stansted

a wall and rural views open up towards some trees on the left. It is initially a hedged track but soon opens up on the right, where a pond can be seen before reaching the church.

St Mary's, Stansted was the original parish church in the grounds of Stansted Hall. However, when the railway arrived, the centre of population moved, so the newer St John's was built and is now the main church in the village (this is passed on the final stage of the first walk in this book). St Mary's is now in the care of the Churches Conservation Trust and is kept locked. The brick tower is unusual and was built along with the porch in 1692 by the then patron, Sir Thomas Middleton.

Stansted Hall can be seen to the left. The Hall broke away from a large estate in 1809, and was purchased by a Miss Ellis on her marriage to Ebenezer Maitland, before being abandoned and rebuilt at the end of the 19th century. The Maitlands moved out of the hall in 1921, and it was sold to J. Arthur Findlay, a noted author of spiritualist works. On his death in 1964, it became the J. Arthur Findlay College for Advancement of Psychic Science. Our route takes us on the track to the right of the church, before passing a cottage, some allotments and the new churchyard, back to the road where we turn **left** onto the pavement, opposite the secondary school.

Walk 16: Elsenham to Stansted

We soon reach the walled garden and the outbuildings of Stansted Hall, before crossing over the motorway and turning **left** onto a lane and a sign welcoming us to Burton End, where there is much less traffic. Enter the village, the only part of the parish of Stansted where Roman remains have been found, and follow the road round to the right. This once peaceful hamlet still maintains an air of peacefulness, despite now being wedged between airport and motorway. Try to shut out the noise and enjoy the thatched and gabled cottages, the barn conversion, village pumps and pub (The *Ash* **[9]** is located about 500 yards after we leave the road).

Continue on the road after the pavements disappear, and ignore the first footpath on the left beside a white painted pump. Instead, turn **left** at a wide gap between Evergreen and Four Winds, beside a black-painted pump. Then turn **left** again at the field beside the privet hedge, into the next field, before turning **right** down to the wood. The path actually runs to the right of the wood, but the Essex Wildlife Trust welcome walkers into Turners Spring, and it is well worth accepting the invitation to follow the path through this mixed deciduous wood running beside Bourne Brook. It is also a site where oxlips (a variety of cowslip local to this area) flower in spring. Over 60 species of birds have been recorded here.

Follow the wide courtesy path through the wood to the bottom, where it narrows and swings round to the right towards the exit at a gate by a large tree. Leave the reserve here, and turn **left** to continue beside the wood in a small natural meadow. Just before the corner, turn **left** to cut through the wood into another field, and keep above a steep woody embankment and Bourne Brook on your right towards the motorway.

At the corner of the field before the ditch separating the field from the motorway, turn **right** down the steep embankment onto a track over the brook at a bridge, after which the wide track climbs steeply again. This stretch can be very muddy at times especially at the bottom, but that clears once you are back in woodland. At the top, turn **left** over the branch railway line to the airport, before following the field edge to the mobile phone mast.

Keep to the left of Durrel's Wood, until the next hedge on your left, where the path turns sharp right - here, turn **left** down the right side of the field to the little wood at the bottom. Cross the bridge and turn **left** onto a wide grassy track, keeping the trees to your left. Go through a gate and stay on the path to the trees just before the motorway, where you turn **right** and follow the line of trees round until just after the end.

Walk 16: Elsenham to Stansted

Here, you cross a stile on your left and follow the waymark direction to the next fence. The path through this meadow is not always clear and the long grass will be wet after rain.

There are two stiles each side of a horse ride to cross to another meadow and a short track beside a house to the road at Fullers End. At Fullers End you have a choice: if you are going on to Broxted and do not wish to visit Elsenham, carry straight on over the road and follow it down to the busy Hall Road, where you turn **left**, passing Elsenham Church in the woods. Then go down to the footpath on the right at Abbotford Bridge, where you can pick up the route in the previous chapter. But if you do wish to return to Elsenham, turn **left** along the lane **taking care (!)** as you cross the railway, and back up the hill to the shops.